Excerpted from Fodor's *France 2000*

Fodor's Travel Publications, Inc.
New York • Toronto • London • Sydney • Auckland
**www.fodors.com/paris**

## Fodor's Pocket Paris

**EDITORS:** Natasha Lesser, Lauren A. Myers

**Editorial Contributors:** Simon Hewitt, Nicola Keegan, Alexander Lobrano, Christopher Mooney, Ian Phillips, Chris Smythe, Rebecca Wolf

**Editorial Production:** Brian Vitunic

**Maps:** David Lindroth, *cartographer;* Rebecca Baer, Bob Blake, *map editors*

**Design:** Fabrizio La Rocca, *creative director;* Lyndell Brookhouse-Gil, *cover design;* Jolie Novak, *photo editor*

**Production/Manufacturing:** Mike Costa

**Cover Photograph:** Bob Krist/Corbis

## Copyright

## Important Tip

Although all prices, opening times, and other details in this book are based on information supplied to us at press time, changes occur all the time in the travel world, and Fodor's cannot accept responsibility for facts that become outdated or for inadvertent errors or omissions. So **always confirm information when it matters,** especially if you're making a detour to visit a specific place.

## Special Sales

Fodor's Travel Publications are available at special discounts for bulk purchases for sales promotions or premiums. Special editions, including personalized covers, excerpts of existing guides, and corporate imprints, can be created in large quantities for special needs. For more information, contact your local bookseller or write to Special Markets, Fodor's Travel Publications, 201 E. 50th Street, New York, NY 10022. Inquiries from Canada should be directed to your local Canadian bookseller or sent to Random House of Canada, Ltd., Marketing Department, 2775 Mattheson Blvd. E, Mississauga, Ontario, L4W 4P7. Inquiries from the United Kingdom should be sent to Fodor's Travel Publications, 20 Vauxhall Bridge Road, London, England SW1V 2SA.

PRINTED IN THE UNITED STATES OF AMERICA

10 9 8 7 6 5 4 3 2 1

# CONTENTS

**On the Road with Fodor's**                                    v

Don't Forget to Write *v*

**Smart Travel Tips**                                          xii

**1    Destination: Paris**                                      1

Paris à la Parisienne 2
Pleasures and Pastimes 6
Quick Tours 7

**2    Exploring Paris**                                          9

From the Arc de Triomphe to the Louvre 11
From the Eiffel Tower to Pont de l'Alma 17
The Faubourg St-Honoré 20
The Grand Boulevards 25
The Marais and the Bastille 30
The Islands and the Latin Quarter 37
From Orsay to St-Germain 44
Montparnasse 49
Montmartre 52

**3    Dining**                                                  58

**4    Lodging**                                                 76

**5    Nightlife and the Arts**                                  90

**6    Outdoor Activities and Sports**                           97

**7    Shopping**                                               100

**French Vocabulary**                                          114

**Index**                                                      120

## Maps

Paris *vi–vii*
Paris with Arrondisse-
  ments *viii–ix*
Paris Métro *x–xi*
Arc de Triomphe
  to Louvre *12–13*
Eiffel Tower to Pont de
  l'Alma *18*
The Faubourg St-Honoré
  *22–23*
The Grand Boulevards *26*

The Marais
  and the Bastille *32–33*
The Islands and the Latin
  Quarter *39*
Orsay to St-Germain *46*
Montparnasse *51*
Montmartre *54*
Paris Dining *62–63*
Paris Lodging *80–81*
Paris Shopping *106–107*

# ON THE ROAD WITH FODOR'S

**E**VERY Y2K TRIP is a significant trip. So if there was
ever a time you needed excellent travel information, it's now.
Acutely aware of that fact, we've
pulled out all stops in preparing
*Fodor's Pocket Paris 2000.* To direct you to the places that are truly
worth your time and money in this
important year, we've rallied the
team of endearingly picky know-
it-alls we're pleased to call our writers. Having seen all corners of Paris,
they're real experts on the subjects
they cover for us. If you knew them,
you'd poll them for tips yourself.

**Simon Hewitt,** who first wrote much
of this book, headed to Paris straight
from studying French and art history at Oxford. He moved to Versailles in 1996 to gain a different
perspective on the French capital.

**Nicola Keegan** was born in Ireland
and raised in Iowa. But after
spending one year at the Sorbonne
university, she knew Paris was
going to be her home forever. She
has now been there 11 years and
has become an expert at finding
her way around Paris.

**Natasha Lesser,** editor of *France
2000,* lived in France, but she always finds something new and
surprising no matter how many
times she returns to the city.

**Alexander Lobrano** has lived in
Paris for 13 years. He writes a
weekly dining column for *Paris
Time Out,* is editor of the *Paris
Zagat's Survey,* and has reported
on French food and restaurants
for many British and American
publications.

**Christopher Mooney** came to Paris
to study French philosophy and
hang out in cafés. A born-again
Epicurean, he herein devotes his efforts to finding the best accomo-
dations in Paris.

**Ian Phillips** found his footing as a
freelance journalist, writing on culture and fashion for publications
in Paris, London, and New York.

## Don't Forget to Write

Keeping a travel guide fresh and
up-to-date is a big job. So we love
your feedback—positive and neg-
ative—and follow up on all sug-
gestions. Contact the Pocket Paris
editor at editors@fodors.com or
c/o Fodor's, 201 East 50th Street,
New York, New York 10022. And
have a wonderful trip!

Karen Cure
*Editorial Director*

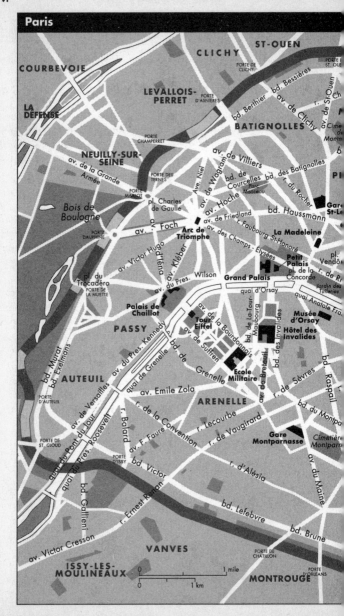

# Paris

ST-OUEN

CLICHY

COURBEVOIE

LEVALLOIS-PERRET

PORTE DE CLICHY

PORTE D'ASNIÈRES

bd. Berthier

av. de Clichy

av. de St-Ch

LA DÉFENSE

BATIGNOLLES

Cime de Monti

PORTE CHAMPERRET

NEUILLY-SUR-SEINE

av. de la Grande Armée

av. de Villiers

bd. des Batignolles

PI

PORTE DES TERNES

Ave. Niel

av. de Wagram

bd. de Courcelles

bd. des Batignolles

r. du Rocher

Gare St-La

PORTE MAILLOT

pl. Charles de Gaulle

av. Hoche

Parc Monceau

bd. Haussmann

Bois de Boulogne

PORTE DAUPHINE

av. Foch

av. de Friedland

La Madeleine

Arc de Triomphe

av. des Champs-Élysées

r. Faubourg St-Honoré

Petit Palais

pl. Vendô

av. Victor Hugo

av. Kléber

av. d'Iéna

Grand Palais

pl. de la Concorde

r. de Ri

pl. du Trocadéro

av. du Prés. Wilson

quai d'Orsay

Jardin des Tuileries

quai Anatole Fra

PORTE DE LA MUETTE

Palais de Chaillot

av. de la Bourdonnais

bd. de la Tour-Maubourg

Musée d'Orsay

Tour Eiffel

Hôtel des Invalides

PASSY

av. du Prés. Kennedy

av. de Suffren

bd. de Grenelle

bd. des Invalides

bd. Murat

bd. Exelmans

quai de Grenelle

Grenelle

École Militaire

av. de Breteuil

r. de Sèvres

bd. Raspail

AUTEUIL

av. de Versailles

av. Emile Zola

GRENELLE

r. Lecourbe

PORTE D'AUTEUIL

r. Balard

r. de la Convention

r. de Vaugirard

Gare Montparnasse

Cimetière Montparn

PORTE DE ST-CLOUD

av. du Pont du Jour

av. F. Faure

Gare Montparnasse

av. du Maine

quai du Prés. Roosevelt

PORTE D'ISSY

bd. Victor

r. d'Alésia

bd. Gallieni

r. Ernest Renan

bd. Lefebvre

bd. Brune

av. Victor Cresson

VANVES

PORTE DE CHATILLON

ISSY-LES-MOULINEAUX

MONTROUGE

PORTE D'ORLÉANS

0          1 mile

0     1 km

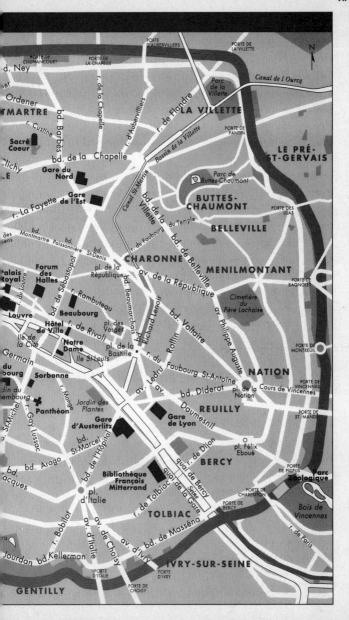

d. Ney
Ordener
MARTRE
r. Custine
Sacré
Coeur
clichy
E
bd. Barbès
Gare du
Nord
r. La Fayette
Gare
de l'Est
des
ens
bd. Montmartre
Poissonnière
bd. St-Denis
Palais
Royal
Forum
des
Halles
bd. de Sébastopol
r. Rambuteau
Louvre
Beaubourg
Hôtel
de Ville
r. de Rivoli
Île
de la Cité
Notre
Dame
Île St-Louis
Germain
du
bourg
Sorbonne
din du
embourg
St-Michel
Gay Lussac
Panthéon
Jardin des
Plantes
Gare
d'Austerlitz
r. St-Marcel
bd. de l'Hôpital
bd. Arago
ris
r. Jacques
Jourdan bd. Kellerman
r. Bobillot
av. de Choisy
av. d'Italie
pl.
d'Italie
Bibliothèque
François
Mitterrand
av. d'Ivry
bd. de Masséna
GENTILLY

PORTE DE
CLIGNANCOURT
PORTE DE
LA CHAPELLE
r. de la Chapelle
r. d'Aubervilliers
PORTE D'AUBERVILLIERS
PORTE DE
LA VILLETTE
Canal de l'Ourcq
N
Parc
de la
Villette
r. de Flandre
LA VILLETTE
bd. de la Chapelle
Bassin de la Villette
PORTE DE
PANTIN
LE PRÉ-
ST-GERVAIS
Canal St-Martin
bd. de la Villette
du Temple
Parc de
Buttes-Chaumont
BUTTES-
CHAUMONT
PORTE DES
LILAS
r. du Faubourg
BELLEVILLE
CHARONNE
pl. de la
République
bd. de Belleville
MENILMONTANT
bd. Beaumarchais
Richard Lenoir
Roquette
bd. Voltaire
av. Philippe Auguste
Cimetière
du
Père Lachaise
PORTE DE
BAGNOLET
pl. des
Vosges
pl. de la
Bastille
r. du Faubourg St-Antoine
av. Ledru-Rollin
av.
bd. Diderot
NATION
pl. de la
Nation
Cours de Vincennes
PORTE DE
MONTREUIL
PORTE DE
VINCENNES
PORTE DE
ST-MANDÉ
Daumesnil
Gare
de Lyon
REUILLY
r. de Dijon
quai de Bercy
quai de la Gare
Seine
BERCY
pl. Félix
Eboué
PORTE
DE PICPUS
Parc
Zoologique
r. de Tolbiac
PORTE DE
CHARENTON
Bois de
Vincennes
TOLBIAC
PORTE
DE BERCY
r. de Paris
PORTE
D'ITALIE
PORTE
D'IVRY
IVRY-SUR-SEINE
PORTE DE
CHOISY

# Paris with Arrondissements

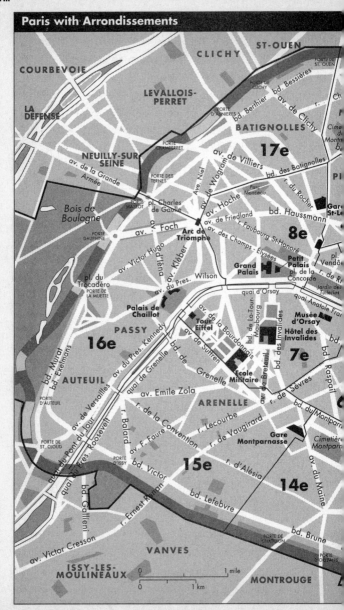

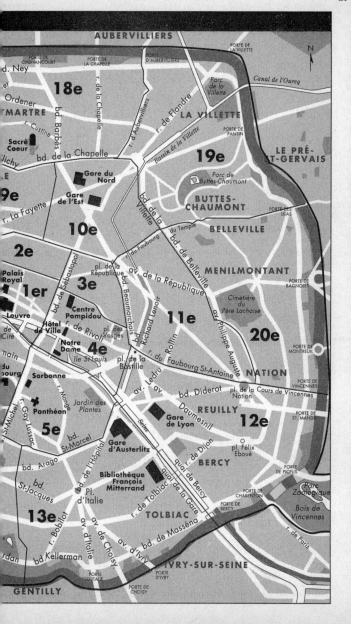

x

# SMART TRAVEL TIPS

## ADDRESSES

Addresses in Paris are fairly straightforward: Each has a number, street name, and, often, the location in one of Paris's 20 arrondissements (for instance, Paris 75010 or, simply, the last two digits, 10ᵉ, both of which indicate that the address is in the 10th). Due to its large size, the 16th arrondissement has two numbers assigned to it: 75016 and 75116. Occasionally you may see an address with a number plus "bis," for instance, 20 bis rue Vavin: This indicates that 20 bis is the next entrance or door down from 20 rue Vavin.

## AIR TRAVEL

Flying time to Paris is 7 hours from New York, 9½ hours from Chicago, and 11 hours from Los Angeles. Flying time from the United Kingdom to Paris is 1½ hours.

### CARRIERS

► MAJOR AIRLINES: **Air France** (☎ 800/237–2747 in the U.S.; 08–02–80–28–02 in France). **American Airlines** (☎ 800/433–7300 in the U.S.; 01–69–32–73–07 in France). **Continental** (☎ 800/231–0856 in the U.S.; 01–42–99–09–09 in France). **Delta** (☎ 800/241–4141 in the U.S.; 01–47–68–92–92 in France). **Northwest** (☎ 800/225–2525 in the U.S., 01–42–66–90–00 in France). **TWA** (☎ 800/892–4141 in the U.S., 08–01–89–28–

92 in France). **United** (☎ 800/538–2929 in the U.S.; 08–01–72–72–72 in France). **US Airways** (☎ 800/428–4322 in the U.S.; 01–49–10–29–00 in France).

► TRAVEL BETWEEN THE U.K. AND FRANCE: **Air France** (☎ 020/8742–6600 in the U.K.; 08–02–80–28–02 in France). **Air U.K.** (☎ 0345/666–777 in the U.K.; 01–44–56–18–08 in France). **British Airways** (☎ 0345/222–111 in the U.K.; 08–02–80–29–02 in France). **British Midland** (☎ 020/8754–7321 or 0345/554–554 in the U.K.; 01–48–62–55–65 in France).

## AIRPORTS & TRANSFERS

Paris's major airports are Charles de Gaulle (also known as Roissy), 26 km (16 mi) northeast of Paris, and Orly, 16 km (10 mi) south of Paris. Paris is accessible from both airports, though only Roissy has a TGV station.

► AIRPORT INFORMATION: **Charles de Gaulle/Roissy** (☎ 01–48–62–22–80 in English). **Orly** (☎ 01–49–75–15–15).

### TRANSFERS

**Charles de Gaulle/Roissy:** From the Charles de Gaulle airport, **the least expensive way to get into Paris is on the RER-B line,** the suburban express train, which leaves from beneath Terminal 2 (look for signs for the RER in the airport terminal;

you may have to catch the free bus to get to the RER station, which is only a short ride away). Trains to central Paris (Les Halles, St-Michel, Luxembourg) depart every 15 minutes. The fare (including métro connection) is 48 francs, and journey time is about 35 minutes. Note that you have to carry your luggage down to the train tracks, and trains can be crowded if you are traveling during rush hour.

Another way to get into Paris is to **take the Air France bus** between Charles de Gaulle airport and the city (you needn't have flown Air France to use this service). Buses run every 12 minutes between the airport and Montparnasse, as well as between the airport and the Arc de Triomphe, with a stop at the Air France air terminal at Porte Maillot. The fare is 55 francs, and journey time is about 40 minutes. Another option is to **take Roissy-bus, operated by the Paris Transit Authority,** which runs between Charles de Gaulle and the Opéra every 15 minutes; the cost is 45 francs. Note that you have to hail the bus that you want—it will not stop automatically—and that rush-hour traffic can make the trip slow.

At the airport, **taxis are readily available.** Journey time is around 30 minutes, depending on the traffic, and the average fare is 150–250 francs; ask what the fare will be before getting in the taxi. Expect to pay a 6-franc supplement per piece of luggage. Another op-

tion is to **arrange a ride with Paris Airports Service or Airport Shuttle,** which can meet you on arrival in a private car and drive you to your destination (about 120 francs for one person, and 89 francs per additional person).

**Orly:** From the Orly airport, **the most economical way to get into Paris is to take the RER-C line;** catch the free shuttle bus from the terminal to the train station. Trains to Paris leave every 15 minutes. The fare is 30 francs, and journey time is about 35 minutes. Another option is to **take the monorail service, Orlyval,** which runs between the Antony RER-B station and Orly airport every 7 minutes. The fare to downtown Paris is 57 francs.

You can also **take an Air France bus** from Orly to Les Invalides on the Left Bank; these run every 12 minutes (you need not have flown on Air France to use this service). The fare is 45 francs, and journey time is between 30 and 45 minutes, depending on traffic. The Paris Transit Authority's **Orlybus is yet another option**; buses leave every 15 minutes for the Denfert-Rochereau métro station; the cost is 30 francs.

In light traffic, **taxis take around 25 minutes from Orly to downtown Paris;** the fare will be about 160 francs. Be sure to ask about the fare before getting in the taxi. With advance reservations, **Paris**

**Airports Service or Airport Shuttle can pick you up at Orly** and drive you directly to your destination. If possible make your Airport Shuttle reservations two to three days in advance; MasterCard and Visa are accepted and the operators speak English. Note that prices depend on the total number of people traveling.

➤ TAXIS & SHUTTLES: **Air France Bus** (☎ 01–41–56–89–00 for recorded information in English). **Airport Shuttle** (☎ 01–45–38–55–72, or toll free from the U.S. 888/426–2705). **Paris Airports Service** (☎ 01–49–62–78–78).

## BUS TRAVEL WITHIN PARIS

Although it's slower than the métro, **traveling by bus is a convenient and scenic way to get around the city.** Paris buses are green and white; route number and destination are marked in front and major stopping-places along the sides. When you want to get off, press the red request button and the *arret demandé* sign will light up. Most routes operate from 7 AM to 8:30 PM; some continue to midnight. Eighteen Noctambus, or night buses, operate hourly (1:30–5:30 AM) between Châtelet and various nearby suburbs; they can be stopped by hailing them at any point on their route.

The brown bus shelters, topped by red and yellow circular signs, contain timetables and route maps. Paris Visite/Mobilis passes (☞ Métro, *below*) are valid, otherwise

it costs 30 francs. Regular buses accept métro tickets, or you can buy a single ticket on board. If you have individual tickets, you should **be prepared to punch one or more tickets in the red and gray machines on board the bus.** You need to show (but not punch) weekly, monthly, and Paris Visite/Mobilis tickets to the driver.

The Balabus, a public bus that runs between May and September, gives an interesting tour around the major sights. Terminus: La Défense or Gare de Lyon.

➤ BUS INFORMATION: **SNCF** (✉ 88 rue St-Lazare, 75009 Paris, ☎ 08–36–35–35–39 in English).

## BUSINESS HOURS

During **weekdays banks are open,** generally 9:30 AM–4:30 or 5 PM (note that the Banque de France closes at 3:30), and some banks are open on Saturday 9–5 as well. In general government offices and businesses are open 9–5.

Most **museums close one day a week**—usually either Monday or Tuesday—and on national holidays. Generally, museums and national monuments are open from 10 AM to 5 or 6 PM. A few close for lunch (noon–2) and are open Sunday only in the afternoon. Many of the large museums have one *nocturne* (nighttime) opening per week when they are open until 9:30 or 10 PM.

Generally, **large shops are open from 9:30 or 10 AM to 6 or 7 PM** and don't close at lunchtime. Many of the large department stores stay open until 10 PM on Wednesday or Thursday. Smaller shops and many supermarkets often open earlier (8 AM) but take a lengthy lunch break (1 PM–3 PM) and generally close around 8 PM; small food shops are often open Sunday mornings, 9 AM–1 PM. Some corner grocery stores stay open until about 10 PM. Most shops close all day Sunday, except some around the Marais, the Bastille, the Latin Quarter, and the Ile de la Cité.

## CAR RENTAL

Rates in Paris begin at approximately $70 a day and $200 a week for an economy car with air-conditioning, manual transmission, and unlimited mileage. This does not include tax on car rentals, which is 20.6% or, if you pick it up at the airport, the airport tax.

➤ MAJOR AGENCIES: **Alamo** (☎ 800/522–9696; 020/8759–6200 in the U.K.). **Avis** (☎ 800/331–1084; 800/879–2847 in Canada; 02/9353–9000 in Australia; 09/525–1982 in New Zealand). **Budget** (☎ 800/527–0700; 0144/227–6266 in the U.K.). **Dollar** (☎ 800/800–6000; 020/8897–0811 in the U.K., where it is known as Euro-dollar; 02/9223–1444 in Australia). **Hertz** (☎ 800/654–3001; 800/263–0600 in Canada; 020/8897–2072 in the U.K.; 02/9669–2444 in Australia; 03/358–6777 in New Zealand). **National Inter-Rent** (☎ 800/227–3876; 0345/

222525 in the U.K., where it is known as Europcar InterRent).

## CAR TRAVEL

### EMERGENCIES

If your car breaks down on an expressway, **go to a roadside emergency telephone.** If you have a breakdown anywhere else, find the nearest garage or contact the police (dial 17).

### GASOLINE

Gas is expensive and prices vary enormously; anything from 5.80 to 6.80 francs per liter.

### PARKING

Finding parking in Paris is very difficult. Meters and ticket machines (pay and display) are common: Make sure you **have a supply of 1-, 2-, 5-, and 10-franc coins.** If you're planning on spending a lot of time in Paris with a car, **it might be a good idea to buy a parking card** (*carte de stationnement*) for 100 francs at any café sporting the red TABAC sign. Note that in August, parking is free in certain residential areas; however, **only parking meters with a dense yellow circle on them indicate free parking in August; if you do not see the circle, pay.** Parking lots, indicated by a blue sign with a white "P," are usually underground and are generally expensive.

### REQUIREMENTS & RESTRICTIONS

In France **your own driver's license is acceptable.** An International Driver's Permit is not necessary unless you are planning on a long-term stay; you can get one from the American or Canadian automobile association, and, in the United Kingdom, from the Automobile Association or Royal Automobile Club.

➤ AUTO CLUBS: **American Automobile Association** (☎ 800/564–6222). **Automobile Association** (☎ 0990/500–600). **Royal Automobile Club** (☎ 0990/722–722 for membership inquiries, 0345/121345 for insurance).

## RULES OF THE ROAD

In France, you drive on the right and **yield to drivers coming from streets to the right.** However, this rule does not necessarily apply at roundabouts, where you should watch out for just about everyone. You must **wear your seat belt,** and children under 12 may not travel in the front seat. Speed limits are 130 kph (80 mph) on expressways, 110 kph (70 mph) on divided highways, 90 kph (55 mph) on other roads, 50 kph (30 mph) in towns.

## CUSTOMS & DUTIES

When shopping, **keep receipts** for all purchases. Upon reentering the country, **be ready to show customs officials what you've bought.** If you feel a duty is incorrect or object to the way your clearance was handled, note the inspector's badge number and ask to see a supervisor. If the problem isn't resolved, write

to the appropriate authorities, beginning with the port director at your point of entry.

### IN CANADA

Canadian residents who have been out of Canada for at least 7 days may bring home C$500 worth of goods duty-free. If you've been away less than 7 days but more than 48 hours, the duty-free allowance drops to C$200; if your trip lasts 24–48 hours, the allowance is C$50. You may not pool allowances with family members. Goods claimed under the C$500 exemption may follow you by mail; those claimed under the lesser exemptions must accompany you. Alcohol and tobacco products may be included in the 7-day and 48-hour exemptions but not in the 24-hour exemption. If you meet the age requirements of the province or territory through which you reenter Canada, you may bring in, duty-free, 1.14 liters (40 imperial ounces) of wine or liquor *or* 24 12-ounce cans or bottles of beer or ale. If you are 16 or older you may bring in, duty-free, 200 cigarettes and 50 cigars. Check ahead of time with Revenue Canada or the Department of Agriculture for policies regarding meat products, seeds, plants, and fruits.

You may send an unlimited number of gifts worth up to C$60 each duty-free to Canada. Label the package UNSOLICITED GIFT—VALUE UNDER $60. Alcohol and tobacco are excluded.

➤ INFORMATION: **Revenue Canada**
(✉ 2265 St. Laurent Blvd. S,
Ottawa, Ontario K1G 4K3,
☎ 613/993–0534; 800/461–9999
in Canada).

### IN FRANCE

If you're coming from outside the
European Union (EU), you may
import duty free: (1) 200 cigarettes
or 100 cigarillos or 50 cigars or
250 grams of tobacco (twice that if
you live outside Europe); (2) 2
liters of wine and, in addition, (a) 1
liter of alcohol over 22% volume
(most spirits) or (b) 2 liters of alcohol under 22% volume (fortified or
sparkling wine) or 2 more liters of
table wine; (3) 50 milliliters of perfume and 250 milliliters of toilet
water; (4) 200 grams of coffee, 100
grams of tea; and (5) other goods
to the value of 300 francs (100
francs for those under 15).

If you're arriving from an EU
country, you may be required to
declare all goods and prove that
anything over the standard limit is
for personal consumption. But
there is no limit or customs tariff
imposed on goods carried within
the EU.

Any amount of French or foreign
currency may be brought into
France, but foreign currencies
converted into francs may be re-
converted into a foreign currency
only up to the equivalent of
5,000 francs.

➤ INFORMATION: **Direction des
Douanes** (✉ 16 rue Yves Toudic,
10ᵉ, ☎ 01–40–40–39–00).

### IN THE U.K.

If you are a U.K. resident and your
journey was wholly within the European Union (EU), you won't
have to pass through customs
when you return to the United
Kingdom. If you plan to bring back
large quantities of alcohol or tobacco, check EU limits beforehand.

➤ INFORMATION: **HM Customs
and Excise** (✉ Dorset House,
Stamford St., Bromley Kent BR1
1XX, ☎ 020/7202–4227).

### IN THE U.S.

U.S. residents who have been out
of the country for at least 48
hours (and who have not used the
$400 allowance or any part of it
in the past 30 days) may bring
home $400 worth of foreign
goods duty-free.

U.S. residents 21 and older may
bring back 1 liter of alcohol duty-
free. In addition, regardless of
your age, you are allowed 200
cigarettes and 100 non-Cuban
cigars. Antiques, which the U.S.
Customs Service defines as objects
more than 100 years old, enter
duty-free, as do original works of
art done entirely by hand.

You may also send packages home
duty-free: up to $200 worth of
goods for personal use, with a
limit of one parcel per addressee
per day (and no alcohol or tobacco
products or perfume worth more
than $5); label the package PER-
SONAL USE and attach a list of its
contents and their retail value. Do

not label the package UNSOLICITED GIFT or your duty-free exemption will drop to $100. Mailed items do not affect your duty-free allowance on your return.

➤ INFORMATION: **U.S. Customs Service** (inquiries, ✉ 1300 Pennsylvania Ave. NW, Washington, DC 20229, ☎ 202/927–6724; complaints, ✉ Office of Regulations and Rulings, 1300 Pennsylvania Ave. NW, Washington, DC 20229; registration of equipment, ✉ Resource Management, 1300 Pennsylvania Ave. NW, Washington, DC 20229, ☎ 202/927–0540).

## DISCOUNT PASSES

Paris Tourist Offices, railroad stations, major métro stations, and participating museums sell the *Carte Musées et Monuments* (Museums and Monuments Pass), which offers unlimited access to more than 65 museums and monuments in Paris over a one-, three-, or five- consecutive day period; the cost, respectively, is 80, 160, and 240 francs. Temporary exhibitions are not included in this pass. This pass is beneficial if you are going to visit many museums and monuments in a short amount of time; also, it may allow you access to museums and monuments without having to wait in line. However, if you don't plan on seeing that many museums or monuments, you may be better off paying per sight. *See also* Métro *and* Train Travel, *below,* for information on métro and train passes.

## ELECTRICITY

To use your U.S.-purchased electric-powered equipment **bring a converter and adapter.** The electrical current in France is 220 volts, 50 cycles alternating current (AC); wall outlets take continental-type plugs, with two round prongs.

If your appliances are dual-voltage you'll need only an adapter. Most laptops operate equally well on 110 and 220 volts and so require only an adapter.

## EMBASSIES

➤ EMBASSY ADDRESSES: **Canada** (✉ 35 av. Montaigne, Paris, 8ᵉ, ☎ 01–44–43–29–00, métro Franklin-D.-Roosevelt, ⊘ weekdays 8:30–11). **United Kingdom** (✉ 35 rue du Faubourg-St-Honoré, Paris, 8ᵉ, ☎ 01–44–51–31–00, métro Madeleine, ⊘ weekdays 9:30–12:30 and 2:30–5). **United States** (✉ 2 rue St-Florentin, Paris, 1ᵉʳ, ☎ 01–43–12–22–22 in English or ☎ 01–43–12–23–47 in emergencies, métro Concorde, ⊘ weekdays 9–3).

## EMERGENCIES

➤ DOCTORS & DENTISTS: **Dentists** (☎ 01–43–37–51–00). **Doctors** (☎ 01–47–07–77–77).

➤ EMERGENCY SERVICES: **Ambulance** (☎ 15 or ☎ 01–45–67–50–50). **Fire Department** (☎ 18). **Police** (☎ 17).

➤ HOSPITALS: **The American Hospital** (✉ 63 bd. Victor Hugo, Neuilly, ☎ 01–46–41–25–25).

**The Hertford British Hospital**
(⊠ 3 rue Barbès, Levallois-Perret,
☎ 01–46–39–22–22).

➤ LATE-NIGHT AND 24-HOUR
PHARMACIES: **Dhéry** (⊠ Galerie
des Champs, 84 av. des Champs-
Élysées, 8ᵉ, ☎ 01–45–62–02–41)
is open 24 hours. **Pharmacie des
Arts** (⊠ 106 bd. Montparnasse,
14ᵉ) is open daily until midnight.
**Pharmacie Matignon** (⊠ rue Jean
Mermoz, at the Rond-Point de
Champs-Élysées, 8ᵉ) is open daily
until 2 AM.

## HOLIDAYS

In May, there is a holiday nearly
every week, so be prepared for
stores, banks, and museums to
shut their doors for days at a time.

January 1 (New Year's Day);
April 3 (Easter Monday); May 1
(Labor Day); May 8 (VE Day);
May 13 (Ascension); May 22
(Pentecost Monday); July 14
(Bastille Day); August 15 (As-
sumption); November 1 (All
Saints); November 11 (Armistice);
December 25 (Christmas).

## MÉTRO

Métro stations are recognizable either by a large yellow *M* within a
circle or by the distinctive curly
green Art Nouveau railings and
archway bearing the full title
(Métropolitain). Taking **the métro
is the most efficient way to get
around Paris.**

Fourteen métro and two RER
(Réseau Express Régional, or the

Regional Express Network) lines
crisscross Paris and the suburbs,
and you are seldom more than 500
yards from the nearest station. The
métro network connects at several
points in Paris with the RER, the
commuter trains that go from the
city center to the suburbs. RER
trains crossing Paris on their way
from suburb to suburb can be great
time-savers because they only make
a few stops in the city (you can use
the same tickets for both the métro
and the RER within Paris).

It's essential to **know the name of
the last station on the line you
take,** as this name appears on all
signs. A connection (you can make
as many as you like on one ticket)
is called a *correspondance*. At
junction stations, illuminated
orange signs bearing the name of
the line terminus appear over the
correct corridors for each correspondance. Illuminated blue signs
marked *sortie* indicate the station
exit. Note that tickets are only
valid inside the gates or *limites*.

Métro service starts at 5:30 AM and
continues until 1:00 AM, when the
last train on each line reaches its
terminus. Some lines and stations
in the less salubrious parts of Paris
are a bit risky at night, in particular
Lines 2 and 13. But in general, the
métro is relatively safe throughout,
providing you **don't walk around
with your wallet hanging out of
your back pocket or (especially
women) travel alone late at night.**

**FARES & SCHEDULES**

All **métro tickets and passes are valid not only for the métro, but also for all RER and bus travel within Paris.** Métro tickets cost 8 francs each; a *carnet* (10 tickets for 52 francs) is a better value.

The advantage of one-day (Mobilis) and three- and five-day (Paris Visite) unlimited travel tickets for the métro, bus, and RER is that, unlike the coupon jaune, which is good from Monday morning to Sunday evening, Mobilis and Paris Visite passes are valid starting any day of the week and also give you discounts on a limited number of museums and tourist attractions. The price is 30 francs (one-day), 80 francs (two-day), 120 francs (three-day), and 175 francs (five-day) for Paris only. Suburbs such as Versailles and St-Germain-en-Laye cost 175 (one-day). Disneyland Paris costs 155, 225, 280, and 357 francs respectively for a one- to four-day pass.

Access to métro and RER platforms is through an automatic ticket barrier. Slide your ticket in and pick it up as it pops out. Be certain to **keep your ticket during your journey;** you'll need it to leave the RER system and in case you run into any green-clad ticket inspectors who will impose a big fine if you can't produce your ticket.

➤ MÉTRO INFORMATION: **RATP** (✉ Pl. de la Madeleine, 8ᵉ; 53 bis quai des Grands-Augustins, 6ᵉ, ☎ 08–36–68–41–14, www.ratp.fr); open daily 9–5.

## MONEY MATTERS

The tourist area where value for money is most difficult to find is the 8ᵉ arrondissement, on and around the Champs-Élysées. Places where you can generally be certain to shop, eat, and stay without overpaying include the streets surrounding Montmartre (not the Butte, or hilltop, itself); the St-Michel/Sorbonne area on the Left Bank; the mazelike streets around Les Halles and the Marais in central Paris; in Montparnasse, south of the boulevard; and the Bastille, République, and Belleville areas of eastern Paris.

In cafés, bars, and some restaurants, two prices are listed, *au comptoir* (at the counter) and *à salle* (at a table), and sometimes a third for the terrace. A cup of coffee, standing at a bar, costs from 7 francs; if you sit, it will cost from 10–40 francs. A glass of beer costs from 10 francs standing and from 15–40 francs sitting; a soft drink costs between 10 francs and 20 francs. A ham sandwich will cost between 17 francs and 30 francs. Expect to pay 20–70 francs for a short taxi ride.

For information on taxes, *see* Taxes, *below.*

**ATMS**

Fairly common in Paris, **ATMs are one of the easiest ways to get francs.** Although ATM transaction fees may be higher abroad than at home, banks usually offer excellent, wholesale exchange rates through ATMs. You may, however, have to look around for Cirrus and Plus locations; it's a good idea to get a list of locations from your bank before you go. Note, too, that you may have better luck with ATMs if you're using a credit card or a debit card that is also a Visa or MasterCard, rather than just your bank card.

To get cash at ATMs in Paris, **your PIN must be four digits long.** Note, too, that you may be charged by your bank for using ATMs overseas; inquire at your bank about charges.

### CREDIT CARDS

Many restaurants and stores take both credit cards and bank debit cards (affiliated with Visa or MasterCard), though there is often a 100-franc minimum.

➤ REPORTING LOST CARDS: American Express (☎ 336/939–1111 or 336/668–5309) call collect. **Diner's Club** (☎ 303/799–1504) call collect. **Mastercard** (☎ 0800/90–1387). **Visa** (☎ 0800/90–1179; collect: 410/581–9994).

### CURRENCY

The units of currency in France are the franc (fr) and the centime. Bills are in denominations of 500, 200, 100, 50, and 20 francs. Coins are 20, 10, 5, 2, and 1 francs and 50, 20, 10, and 5 cen-

times. Pay close attention to the one hundred and two hundred franc notes as they can be easily confused. At press time (1999), the exchange rate was about 6.1 francs to the U.S. dollar, 4.2 to the Canadian dollar, 10 to the pound sterling, 4 to the Australian dollar, 3.4 to the New Zealand dollar, and 8.3 to the Irish punt.

The euro, or single European currency, was launched on January 1, 1999. One euro equals 6.55 francs. At the moment, the euro functions as an alternative currency, but by 2002 it will replace the national currencies of eleven of the fifteen countries in the European Union. Prices on all items from coffee to cars are now listed in euros as well as francs.

### CURRENCY EXCHANGE

These days, **the easiest way to get francs is through ATMs** (☞ *above*); you can find them in airports, train stations, and throughout the city. It's a good idea, however, to bring some francs with you from home and to always have some cash and traveler's checks as back up. For the best deal, **compare rates at banks and booths** and **look for exchange booths that clearly state "no commission."** At exchange booths always confirm the rate with the teller before exchanging money. You won't do as well at exchange booths in airports or rail and bus stations, in hotels, in restaurants, or in stores. Of all the banks in Paris, **Banque de France generally has the best rates.**

➤ EXCHANGE SERVICES: International Currency Express (☎ 888/842–0880 on East Coast; 888/278–6628 on West Coast). **Thomas Cook Currency Services** (☎ 800/287–7362).

### TRAVELER'S CHECKS

Although you can get francs from ATMs, you may also want to **bring some money in traveler's checks, just in case.** The benefit of traveler's checks is that lost or stolen checks can usually be replaced within 24 hours. To ensure a speedy refund, buy your own traveler's checks—don't let someone else pay for them. Traveler's checks in dollars or other currencies can easily be exchanged at banks or exchange bureaus, though you need your passport to do this.

## PASSPORTS & VISAS

When traveling in France, **you need to have a passport.** All citizens of Canada, the United States, and the United Kingdom, even infants, need only a valid passport to enter France for stays of up to 90 days.

### PASSPORT OFFICES

➤ CONTACTS: **Canadian Passport Office** (☎ 819/994–3500 or 800/567–6868). **United Kingdom Passport Office, London** (☎ 0990/210–410) for fees and documentation requirements and to request an emergency passport. **United States National Passport Information Center** (☎ 900/225–5674; calls are 35¢ per minute for automated service, $1.05 per minute for operator service).

## TAXES

All taxes must be included in affixed prices in France. Prices in **restaurants and hotel prices must by law include taxes and service charges:** If these appear as additional items on your bill, you should complain. VAT (value-added tax, known in France as TVA), at a standard rate of 20.6% (33% for luxury goods), is included in the price of many goods, but **foreigners are often entitled to a refund.**

### VALUE-ADDED TAX (V.A.T.)

**Global Refund** is a V.A.T. refund service that makes getting your money back hassle-free. Global Refund services are offered in more than 130,000 shops worldwide. In participating stores, ask for a **Global Refund Cheque** when making a purchase—this Cheque will clearly state the amount of your refund in local currency, with the service charge already incorporated (the service charge equals approximately 3%–4% of the purchase price of the item). Global Refund can also process other customs forms, though for a higher fee. When leaving the European Union, get your Global Refund Cheque and any customs forms stamped by the customs official.

You can take them to the cash refund office at the airport, where your money will be refunded right there in cash, by check, or a refund to your credit card. Alternatively, you can mail your validated Cheque to Global Refund, and your credit card account will automatically be credited within three billing cycles.

➤ VAT REFUNDS: **Global Refund** (✉ 707 Summer St., Stamford, CT 06901, ☎ 800/566–9828).

## TAXIS

Daytime rates, A (7 AM–7 PM), within Paris are 3.53 francs per kilometer, and nighttime rates, B, are around 5.83 francs per kilometer. Suburban zones and airports, C, are 7.16 per kilometer. There is a basic hire charge of 13 francs for all rides, a 6-franc supplement per piece of luggage, and a 5-franc supplement if you're picked up at a SNCF station. Waiting time is charged at 130 francs per hour.

## TELEPHONES

### COUNTRY & AREA CODES

The country code for France is 33. The first two digits of French numbers are a prefix determined by zone: Paris and Ile-de-France, 01; the northwest, 02; the northeast, 03; the southeast, 04; and the southwest, 05.

Note that **when dialing France from abroad, drop the initial 0 from the telephone number** (all numbers listed in this book include the initial 0, which is used for calling numbers *in* France). To call a telephone number in Paris from the United States, dial 011–33 plus the phone number minus the initial 0. To call France from the United Kingdom, dial 00–33, then dial the number in France minus the initial 0.

### INTERNATIONAL CALLS

To make a direct international call out of France, dial 00 and wait for the tone, then dial the country code (1 for the United States and Canada, 44 for the United Kingdom) and the area code (minus any initial 0) and number. Expect to be overcharged if you make calls from your hotel. Approximate daytime rates, per minute, are 2.25 francs to the United States and Canada (8:00 AM–9:30 PM), and 2.10 francs for the United Kingdom (2:00 PM–8:00 PM).

To call home with the help of an operator, dial 00–33 plus the country code. There is an automatic 44.5 franc service charge.

Telephone cards (☞ *below*) are sold that enable you to make long-distance and international calls from pay phones.

➤ ACCESS CODES: **AT&T Direct** (☎ 08–00–99–00–11 or 08–00–99–01–11; 800/874–4000 for information). **MCI Call USA** (☎ 08–00–99–00–19; 800/444–4444 for information). **Sprint Express** (☎ 08–00–99–00–87; 800/793–1153 for information).

## LOCAL CALLS

When making a local call in Paris or to Ile-de-France, **dial the full 10-digit number, including the initial 0.** A local call costs 74 centimes for every three minutes.

## PUBLIC PHONES

Most **French pay phones are operated by** *télécartes* (phone cards), which you can buy from post offices, tabacs, and métro stations. These phone cards will save you money and hassle, since it's hard to find phones that take change these days. There are two types of cards: the *télécarte international,* which allows you to make local calls and offers greatly reduced rates on international calls (instructions are in English and the cost is 50 francs for 60 units and 100 francs for 120 units); and the simple *télécarte,* which allows you to make calls in France (the cost is 49 francs for 50 units; 97.5 francs for 120 units). You can also use your credit card in much the same way as a télécarte, but be careful—it's much more expensive.

## TIPPING

Bills in bars and restaurants must, by law, include service, but **it is customary to round out your bill with some small change** unless you're dissatisfied. The amount varies— from 50 centimes or 1 franc for a beer to 10 or 15 francs after a meal. In expensive restaurants, it's common to leave an additional 5% of the bill on the table.

Tip taxi drivers and hairdressers about 10% of the bill. Washroom attendants usually get 2 francs, though the sum is often posted. If you stay more than two or three days in a hotel, it is customary to leave something for the chambermaid—about 10 francs per day. Expect to pay about 10 francs (5 francs in a moderately priced hotel) to the person who carries your bags or who hails you a taxi.

## TRAIN TRAVEL

The SNCF, France's rail system, is fast, punctual, comfortable, and comprehensive. There are various options: local trains, overnight trains with sleeping accommodations, and the high-speed TGV, or *Trains à Grande Vitesse* (averaging 255 kph/160 mph on the Lyon/southeast line, and 300 kph/190 mph on the Lille and Bordeaux/southwest lines).

The TGV, the fastest way to get around the country, operate between Paris and Lille/Calais, Paris and Lyon/Switzerland/the Riviera, Paris and Angers/Nantes, Paris and Tours/Poitiers/Bordeaux, Paris and Brussels, and Paris and Amsterdam. As with other main-line trains, a small supplement may be assessed at peak hours.

Paris has six international rail stations: Gare du Nord (northern France, northern Europe, and England via Calais or Boulogne); Gare St-Lazare (Normandy, England via Dieppe); Gare de l'Est

(Strasbourg, Luxembourg, Basel, and central Europe); Gare de Lyon (Lyon, Marseille, the Riviera, Geneva, Italy); and Gare d'Austerlitz (Loire Valley, southwest France, Spain). Note that Gare Montparnasse has taken over as the main terminus for trains bound for southwest France since the introduction of the new TGV-Atlantique service.

### BETWEEN THE U.K. AND FRANCE

Short of flying, the "Chunnel" is the fastest way to cross the English Channel: 3 hours from London's central Waterloo Station to Paris's central Gare du Nord, 35 minutes from Folkestone to Calais, and 60 minutes from motorway to motorway. Round-trip tickets range from 3,400 francs for first class to 690 francs for second class.

### FARES, SCHEDULES, & RESERVATIONS

You can **call for train information or reserve tickets in any Paris station,** irrespective of destination. If you know what station you'll depart from, you can get a free schedule there (while supplies last), or you can access the new multilingual computerized schedule information network at any Paris station. You can also make reservations and buy your ticket while at the computer. Go to the Grandes Lignes counter for travel within France and to the Billets Internationaux desk if you're heading out of the country. Note that

calling the SNCF's 08 number (☞ *below*) will cost you money (you're charged per minute), so it's better just to go to the nearest station and make reservations.

**Seat reservations are required on TGVs,** and are a good idea on trains that may be crowded—particularly in summer and holidays on popular routes. You also need a reservation for sleeping accommodations.

➤ TRAIN INFORMATION: **BritRail Travel** (☎ 800/677–8585 in the U.S.; 020/7834–2345 in the U.K.). **Eurostar** (☎ 08–36–35–35–39 in France; 0345/881881 in the U.K., www.eurostar.com). **InterCity Europe** (⊠ Victoria Station, London, ☎ 020/7834–2345, 020/7828–0892 or 0990/848–848 for credit-card bookings). **Rail Europe** (☎ 800/942–4866 in the U.S., www.raileurope.com). **SNCF** (⊠ 88 rue St-Lazare, 75009 Paris, ☎ 08–36–35–35–35, www.sncf.fr).

## VISITOR INFORMATION

➤ FRANCE TOURISM OFFICES: **France On-Call** (☎ 410/286–8310 Mon.–Fri. 9–7, www.france-tourism.com). **Chicago** (⊠ 676 N. Michigan Ave., Chicago, IL 60611, fgto@mcs.net). **Los Angeles** (⊠ 9454 Wilshire Blvd., Suite 715, Beverly Hills, CA 90212, fgto@gte.net). **New York City** (⊠ 444 Madison Ave., 16th floor, New York, NY 10022, info@francetourism.com). **Canada** (⊠ 1981 Ave. McGill College,

Suite 490, Montréal, Québec H3A
2W9). **U.K.** (⊠ 178 Piccadilly,
London W1V OAL, ☎ 171/6399–
3500, FAX 171/6493–6594).

➤ LOCAL TOURIST INFORMATION:
**Espace du Tourisme d'Ile-de-
France** (⊠ Carrousel du Louvre,
99 rue de Rivoli, 75001, ☎ 08–
03–81–80–00 or 01–44–50–19–
98). **Office du Tourisme de la Ville
de Paris** (⊠ Paris Tourist Office,
127 av. des Champs-Élysées, ☎
01–49–52–53–54 or 01–49–52–
53–56 for recorded information in
English).

## WHEN TO GO

The major tourist season in France
stretches from Easter to mid-
September, but **Paris has much to
offer in every season.** Paris in the
early spring can be disappoint-
ingly damp, though it's relatively
tourist free; May and June are delightful, with good weather and
plenty of cultural and other attractions. July and August can be sul-
try. Moreover, many theaters and
some of the smaller restaurants
and shops close for at least four
weeks in August. If you're unde-
terred by the hot weather and the
pollution, you'll notice a fairly re-
laxed atmosphere around the city,
as this is the month when most
Parisians are on vacation. September is ideal. Cultural life revives
after the summer break, and
sunny weather often continues
through the first half of October.
The ballet and theater are in full
swing in November, but the
weather is part wet and cold, part
bright and sunny. December is
dominated by the *fêtes de fin d'an-
née* (end-of-year festivities), and a
busy theater, ballet, and opera season into January.

### CLIMATE IN PARIS
What follow are the average daily
maximum and minimum tempera-
tures for Paris.

| Jan. | 43F | 6C | May | 68F | 20C | Sept. | 70F | 21C |
|------|-----|-----|------|-----|-----|-------|-----|-----|
|      | 34  | 1   |      | 49  | 10  |       | 53  | 12  |
| Feb. | 45F | 7C  | June | 73F | 23C | Oct.  | 60F | 16C |
|      | 34  | 1   |      | 55  | 13  |       | 46  | 8   |
| Mar. | 54F | 12C | July | 76F | 25C | Nov.  | 50F | 10C |
|      | 39  | 4   |      | 58  | 14  |       | 40  | 5   |
| Apr. | 60F | 16C | Aug. | 75F | 24C | Dec.  | 44F | 7C  |
|      | 43  | 6   |      | 58  | 14  |       | 36  | 2   |

# 1 Destination: Paris

# PARIS À LA PARISIENNE

**I**T IS MIDNIGHT at the neighborhood brasserie. Waiters swathed in starchy white glance discreetly at their watches as a family—mother, son, and wife—sip the last of a bottle of Chiroubles and scrape up the remains of their steak tartare on silverware dexterously poised with arched wrists. They are all wearing scarves: The mother's is a classic silk *carré,* tastefully folded at the throat; the wife's is Indian gauze and glitters; the son's is wool and hangs like a prayer shawl over his black turtleneck. Finished, they stir their coffee without looking. They smoke: the mother, Gitanes; the son, Marlboros; the wife rolls her own from a silver case. Alone, they act out their personal theater, uncontrived and unobserved, their Doisneauesque tableau reflected only in the etched-glass mirrors around them, enhanced by the sobriety of their dress and the pallor of their Gallic skin.

Whoever first said that "God found Paris too perfect, so he invented the Parisians," had it wrong. This extraordinary maquette of a city, with its landscape of mansards and chimneys, its low-slung bridges and vast boulevards, is nothing but a rough-sketched stage set that drinks its color from the lifeblood of those infamous Parisians whom everyone claims to hate, but whom everyone loves to emulate.

Mythologized for their arrogance, charm, and savoir faire—as well as their disdain for the foreigners they find genetically incapable of sharing these characteristics—the Parisians continue to mesmerize. For the generations of American and English voyeurs who have ventured curiously, enviously into countless mirrored brasseries, downed numerous bottles of *cuvée maison,* fumbled at nautical knots in newly bought scarves, even suffered squashed berets and unfiltered Gauloises, the Parisian remains inimitable—and infinitely fascinating.

Alternately patronizing and self-effacing, they move through their big-city lives with enviable style and urban grit. They are chronically thin, despite the truckloads of beef stew, pâté, and *tarte Tatin* they consume without blushing. They still make the cigarette look glamorous—and a graceful bit of stage business indispensable to good talk—in spite of the gas-mask levels of smoke they generate. They stride over bridges aloof to the monuments framed in every sweeping perspective, yet they discourse—lightly, charmingly—on Racine, NATO, and the latest ruling of the Académie Française. They are proud, practical, often witty and always chic, from the thrift-shop style of the Sorbonne student to the Chanel suit on the thin shoulders of a well-boned *dame d'un certain âge*.

Ferociously (with some justice) in love with their own culture—theater, literature, film, art, architecture, haute cuisine, and haute couture—Parisians worship France as ardently as New Yorkers dismiss the rest of America. While Manhattanites berate the nonentities west of the Hudson, Parisians romanticize the rest of France, making an art of the weekend foray and the regional vacation: Why should we go *à l'étranger* (abroad) when we have the Dordogne, the Auvergne, and Bretagne?

And for all their vulnerability to what they frame as the "American Assault," for every Disney store, action film, and McDonald's in Paris (not to mention Benetton and Laura Ashley, and France's own Celio, Orcade, and Descamps chains), there is a plethora of unique shops selling all-white blouses, African bracelets, dog jackets, and Art Deco jewelry.

And for every commercial bookstore chain there are five tiny *librairies* selling tooled-leather encyclopedias, collections of out-of-print plays, and yellow paperbacks lovingly pressed in waxed paper. The famous *bouquinistes* hover like squatters along the Seine, their folding metal boxes opening to showcase a treasure trove of old magazines, scholarly journals, and hand-colored botanical prints that flap from clothespins in the wind. Yet they are not nomads, these bouquinistes: Dormant through winter, their metal stands are fixtures as permanent and respectable as those of the medieval merchants that built shops along the Pont Neuf. They are determinedly Parisian—individual, independent, and one-of-a-kind.

**B**UT IN SPITE of their fierce individuality, Parisians also demand that certain conformities be followed. And here the gap between native and visitor widens. If Parisians treat tourists a bit like occupying forces—disdainfully selling them Beaujolais-Nouveau in July, seating them by the kitchen doors, refusing to understand honest attempts at French—they have formed their opinions based on bitter experience. The waiter who scorches tourists with flared nostrils and firmly turned back was trained to respect his métier—meaning not pouring Coke with foie gras or bringing the check with dessert. The meal is a sacred ritual here and diverging from the norm is tantamount to disgrace.

Doing as the Parisians do, you can go a long way toward closing the gap of disdain. When dining, for example, give yourself over to the meal. Order a kir as an aperitif, instead of a whiskey or beer. Drink wine or mineral water with your meal. Order coffee *after* dessert, not with it. And accept the fact that diet sodas are rarely available in restaurants.

**T**HE WINE will come chilled, aired, and ready for tasting with the respect usually reserved for a holy relic. Enjoy each course, sipping, discussing, digesting leisurely; the waiter will not be pressed by hurried tourists. When you're done eating, align your silverware on the plate (a sign for the waiter to clear). Cheese can be the climax of the meal, well worth skipping dessert if necessary, and a magnificent way to finish the wine. Have your coffee, without exception, black with sugar; a milky froth will not do on a full stomach. The art of stirring *un express* in Paris rivals the art of scarf-tying.

Ask for *l'addition;* the waiter will not commit the gaffe of bringing the check uninvited. And no matter how deeply you enter into your role as Parisian manqué, avoid saying "Garçon!" (Say "S'il vous plaît" instead.) These are rules that apply at the most unassuming corner bistro and the grandest three-star restaurant; following them can thaw the waiterly chill that can render a meal unforgettable—for all the wrong reasons—and can make for meals that are memorable as an evening at the Opéra de la Bastille, complete with sets and choreography.

It is this fixed attention to experience and detail that sets the Parisians apart. Desk-eaters they are not: When they work, they work without a coffee break. When they eat, business still grinds to a halt. Weekends are sacred. And oh, do they vacation, all of them at once, all of them abandoning Paris in August with a fierceness of purpose that mirrors their commitment to food—an all-night drive, a rental booked months in advance.

By matching that Parisian passion for the complete, the correct, the comme il faut, your own experience will be all the more authentic. Having eaten with proper reverence, keep your sightseeing agenda at the same lofty level. If you go to the Louvre, spend the day; do not lope through the wide corridors in search of *La Joconde* (Mona Lisa). You can leave for a three-hour lunch, if you choose, and come back with the same ticket, even avoiding the lines by reentering via the Passage Richelieu. If time won't allow an all-day survey, do as the locals do: Choose an era and immerse yourself. Then take a break and plunge into another. Eavesdrop on a guided tour. Go back and look at a painting again. And take the time to stare at the ceilings: The architecture alone of this historic monument merits a day's tour.

As you apply yourself to the Parisian experience in spirit, diverge in fact: Walk. The natives may prefer to sit in a café or even hurry straight home by métro (*"métro, boulot, dodo"*—"métro, work, sleep"—as the saying goes). You, as a visitor, are obliged to wander down tortuous medieval streets; up vast boulevards so overscaled you seem to gain no ground; over bridges that open up broad perspectives on illuminated monuments that outnumber even those in Rome.

They are all there, the clichés of Paris romance: The moon over the Seine reflected in the wake of the Bateaux Mouches; the steps Leslie Caron blushed down in *an American in Paris;* the lovers kissing under the lime tree pollards. But there are surprises, too: a troop of hunting horns striking unearthly sonorities under a resonant bridge; flocks of wild geese flying low over the towers of Notre-Dame; and a ragged expatriate-writer leaving a well-scraped plat du jour on the table as he bolts away from the bill. (*accessed doomage:* He would have been well-fed by Reagan, the baker-writer in *acarina de Bergerac* who opened his Paris pastry shop to starving poets.)

The more resourceful you are, the more surprises you will unearth in your Paris wanderings. Follow the strains of Lully into a chamber orchestra rehearsal in St-Julien-le-Pauvre; if you're quiet and still, you may not be asked to leave. Brave the smoking lounge at intermission at the Comédie-Française and you'll find the battered leather chair that the young actor Molière sat in as *L'Invalide Imaginaire*. Take the métro to *L'Armée du Salut* (Salvation Army) in the 13e arrondissement, and you'll not only find Art Deco percolators and hand-knit stockings, but you'll also be inside the futuristic curves of a 1933 Le Corbusier masterwork.

Tear yourself away from the big-name museums and you'll discover a world of small galleries. Go in: You don't have to press your nose to the glass. The exhibits are constantly changing and you can always find one relevant to Paris— Frank Horvat's photos of Pigalle or a Christo retrospective, including the Pont Neuf wrappings. It is worth buying one of the weekly guides—*Pariscope, Les Officiels des Spectacles, Figaroscope*—and browsing through it over your *café crème* and croissant.

**R**ESOURCEFULNESS, after all, is a sign of enthusiasm and appreciation—for when you are well-informed and acutely tuned in to the nuances of the city, you can approach it as a connoisseur. Then you can peacefully coexist with Parisians, partaking, in their passion for this marvelous old city, from the same plate of cultural riches. Hemingway, as usual, put it succinctly: "It was always pleasant crossing bridges in Paris." Cultural bridges, too.

*Bon séjour à Paris.*

— Nancy Coons

A frequent contributor to Fodor's, Nancy Coons has written on food and culture for *National Geographic Traveler*, *Wall Street Journal*, *Opera News*, and *European Travel & Life*. Based in Luxembourg and France since 1987, she now works out of her 300-year-old farmhouse in Lorraine, which she shares with her husband and two daughters.

## Pleasures and Pastimes

### Cafés

People-watching, some would say, is what Paris is all about; and there's no better place to indulge in this pursuit than the terrace of a sidewalk café. Favored locales include Place St-Michel, boulevard du Montparnasse, and Place St-Germain-des-Prés, on the Left Bank; and Place de l'Opéra, the Champs-Élysées, and Les Halles, on the Right Bank. But you may enjoy seeking out your own (less expensive) local haunts.

### Churches

Paris is rich in churches of two architectural styles: the 15th- to 16th-century overlap of Flamboyant Gothic and Renaissance (at St-Gervais, St-Étienne du Mont, St-Eustache, and St-Séverin) and 17th-century Baroque with domes and two-tiered facades (at Les Invalides, Val de Grâce, and St-Paul–St-Louis). But the city's most enduring religious symbols are medieval (Notre-Dame Cathedral and Ste-Chapelle) and 19th-century (Sacré-Coeur and La Madeleine).

### Dining

Paris is one of the world's great food capitals and a bastion of classic French cuisine. Nonetheless, if you're coming from New York, London, or Los Angeles, where innovative restaurants abound, you may find the French capital a little staid. In fact, a battle is currently being waged between the traditionalists and a remarkable new generation of chefs who are modernizing French cooking—and changing the French culinary landscape.

### Museums

Paris has a plethora of museums. Alongside the superstars—the Louvre, the Musée d'Orsay, and the newly renovated Centre Pompidou—are such delights as the

Cité des Sciences at the Parc de La Villette, the Musée National du Moyen Age (displaying medieval works of art), and single-artist museums dedicated to the works of Picasso, Rodin, Dalí, and Maillol.

## Shopping

Shopping opportunities in Paris are endless and geared to every taste. You can spend an afternoon browsing through bookstalls along the Seine, shopping for one of Hermès's famous *foulards* (scarves), touring high-gloss department stores, or bargaining over prices in the sprawling flea markets on the outskirts of town. Everywhere you turn, tastefully displayed wares—luscious chocolates, exquisite clothing, gleaming copper pots—entice the eye and awaken the imagination.

## Quick Tours

If you're here for just a short stay you need to plan carefully so as to make the most of your time in Paris. The following itineraries outline major sights throughout the city, and will help you structure your visit efficiently. Each is intended to take about four hours—perfect to fill a free morning or afternoon. For more information about individual sights, *see* Chapter 2.

### Arc de Triomphe to the Louvre

Start at the **Arc de Triomphe;** from the top there's a great view of the city and the boulevards emanating from the Étoile. With the arch as your starting point, the rest of your walk will be all downhill. Work your way along the **Champs-Élysées,** across **place de la Concorde** and the **Tuileries Garden** (with the notable **Orangerie** and **Jeu de Paume** museums if you have an hour to spare) to the **Louvre.** Note that a tour of the Louvre's galleries could easily take half a day on its own.

### Eiffel Tower and the Musée d'Orsay

West of the École Militaire métro stop, the verdant expanse of the **Champ de Mars** provides a thrilling approach to the **Tour Eiffel.** After you ascend the famous tower (early morning is best to avoid crowds), you can easily spend the rest of a morning or afternoon admiring the vast holdings of the **Musée d'Orsay.** To get to the museum from the Eiffel Tower, walk east along the Seine to the Pont de l'Alma station and take the RER two stops to the Musée d'Orsay.

### The Grand Boulevards

For *très chic* shopping and a look at Haussmann's 19th-century Paris, walk down the Right Bank's **Faubourg St-Honoré** from the Miromesnil or Concorde métro stations. Turn left (north) on rue Royale and join the Grand Boulevards by the **Madeleine** church; continue northeast along the boulevards past the **Opéra Garnier** toward **place de la République.**

## The Left Bank

From the Cluny–La Sorbonne métro stop, explore the **Latin Quarter.** You can stroll around the academic center of Paris, near the **Sorbonne,** and then walk along boulevard St-Michel. If you walk south, the boulevard will take you to the **Panthéon** (via rue Soufflot) and the **Jardin du Luxembourg.** To the north boulevard St-Michel crosses a main artery—boulevard St-Germain—before it ends at place St-Michel and the Seine. For a look at some worthwhile shops and galleries and an open-air food market (on rue de Buci), walk west along boulevard St-Germain toward the Odéon métro stop, then turn north or south onto one of several enticing narrow and winding roads.

## Montmartre

Take the métro to Anvers and head up bustling rue de Steinkerque; the **Sacré-Coeur Basilica** looms overhead. Take the funicular to the top. Walk west through **place du Tertre** and along rue Lepic. Then head south along rue Tholozé to rue des Abbesses and **place des Abbesses,** where you'll find two gems of Art Nouveau: the church St-Jean de Montmartre, and the famous Guimard entrance to the Abbesses métro station.

## Notre-Dame, the Islands, and the Marais

Begin your tour on **Ile de la Cité** with a visit to **Notre-Dame Cathedral** and, if you enjoy medieval architecture, the **Ste-Chapelle** to the east. Head back toward Notre-Dame, then cross the Seine at Pont Louis and wander around village-like **Ile St-Louis,** using rue de St-Louis-en-l'Ile as your main axis. If you've still got some time left, backtrack west to Pont Louis-Philippe and walk north to the Marais via rue du Pont Louis-Philippe and rue Vieille du Temple.

# 2 Exploring Paris

Revised
and
updated by
Simon
Hewitt

**A** CITY OF VAST, NOBLE PERSPECTIVES and winding, hidden streets, Paris remains a combination of the pompous and the intimate. Whether you've come looking for sheer physical beauty, cultural and artistic diversions, world-famous dining and shopping, history, or simply local color, you will find it here in abundance.

For visitors Paris is a practical city: It is relatively small as capitals go, with many of its major sites and museums within walking distance of one another. The city is divided into 20 *arrondissements* (districts). The last two digits of the zip code (e.g., 75002) will tell you the arrondissement (the 2ᵉ, or 2nd). The city's principal tourist axis is less than 6½ km (4 mi) long, running parallel to the north bank of the Seine between the Arc de Triomphe and the Bastille. In fact, the best method of getting to know Paris is on foot, although public transportation—particularly the métro system—is excellent. Buy a *Plan de Paris* booklet, a city map and guide with a street-name index that also shows métro stations. Note that all métro stations have a detailed neighborhood map just inside the entrance.

Paris owes both its development and much of its visual appeal to the Seine River weaving through its heart. Each bank of the Seine has its own personality; the Rive Droite (Right Bank), with its spacious boulevards and formal buildings, generally has a more genteel feel than the carefree Rive Gauche (Left Bank), to the south. The historical and geographical center of Paris is Notre-Dame Cathedral, on the Ile de la Cité, the larger of the city's two islands (the other is the Ile St-Louis).

Our coverage of Paris is divided into nine neighborhood walks. There are several must-sees that you don't want to miss: the Eiffel Tower, the Arc de Triomphe, the Louvre, and Notre-Dame. A few monuments and museums close for lunch, between noon and 2, and many are closed on either Monday or Tuesday: Check before you set off. Admission prices listed are for adults, but often there are special rates for students, children, and senior citizens.

# From the Arc de Triomphe to the Louvre

The Arc de Triomphe stands foursquare at the top of the city's most famous avenue: the Champs-Élysées. Site of most French national celebrations, the Champs-Élysées is the last leg of the Tour de France bicycle race on the third or fourth Sunday in July and the site of vast ceremonies on Bastille Day (July 14) and Armistice Day (November 11). Explore both its commercial upper half and its verdant lower section, which slopes down gracefully to Place de la Concorde, with its Egyptian obelisk. Beyond lie the Tuileries Garden and the gleaming glass pyramid of the world's largest museum, the Louvre. Local charm is not a feature of this exclusive sector of western Paris; it's beautiful, grand—and a little impersonal. The French moan that it's losing its character, and as you notice the number of fast-food joints along the Champs-Élysées, you'll know what they mean—though renovation has gone some way to restoring the avenue's legendary elegance.

*Numbers in the margin correspond to numbers on the Arc de Triomphe to Louvre map; these numbers indicate a suggested path for sightseeing.*

## Sights to See

★ ❸ **Arc de Triomphe.** This huge arch, standing 164 ft, was planned by Napoléon but not finished until 1836, 20 years after the end of his rule. It is decorated with some magnificent sculpture by François Rude, such as the *Departure of the Volunteers,* better known as *La Marseillaise,* to the right of the arch when viewed from the Champs-Élysées. A small museum halfway up the arch is devoted to its history. France's Unknown Soldier is buried beneath the archway; the flame is rekindled every evening at 6:30. ⊠ *Pl. Charles-de-Gaulle,* ☎ *01–43–80–31–31.* ☎ *35 frs.* ☉ *Spring–autumn, daily 9:30 AM–11 PM; winter, daily 10 AM–10:30 PM. Métro, RER: Étoile.*

❶ **Bois de Boulogne** (Boulogne Woods). Class and style have been associated with this 2,200-acre park—known to Parisians as "Le Bois"—ever since it was landscaped into an upper-class playground by Baron Haussmann in the 1850s. That onetime glamour is emphasized by Haussmann's approach road from the Arc de Triomphe: avenue

**12**

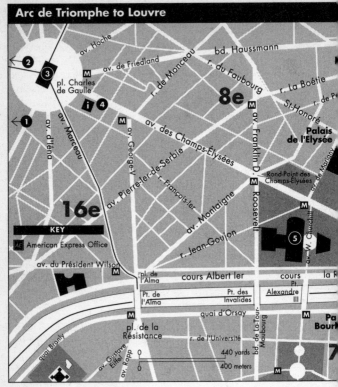

## Arc de Triomphe to Louvre

*(Map labels:)*

av. Hoche
bd. Haussmann
av. de Friedland
r. de Manceau
r. du Faubourg
r. La Boétie
r. de Pe
pl. Charles de Gaulle
8e
St-Honoré
Palais de l'Elysée
av. d'Iéna
av. Marceau
av. George-V
av. des Champs-Élysées
av. Franklin D. Roosevelt
Rond-Point des Champs-Élysées
av. de Marign
av. Pierre-1er-de-Serbie
r.-François-1er
16e
av. Montaigne
r. Jean-Goujon
av. de W. Churchill

**KEY**

**AE** American Express Office

av. du Président Wilson
pl. de l'Alma
cours Albert 1er
cours
la R
Pt. de l'Alma
Pt. des Invalides
Alexandre III
Pt
quai d'Orsay
bd. de La-Tour-Maubourg
Pa
Bour
pl. de la Résistance
r. de l'Université
7
quai Branly
av. Gustave-Eiffel
av. Rapp

0      440 yards
0      400 meters

Arc de Triomphe, **3**

Bois de Boulogne, **1**

La Défense, **2**

Grand Palais, **5**

Jardin des Tuileries, **9**

Louvre, **10**

Musée du Jeu de Paume, **7**

Musée de l'Orangerie, **8**

Office de Tourisme de la Ville de Paris, **4**

Place de la Concorde, **6**

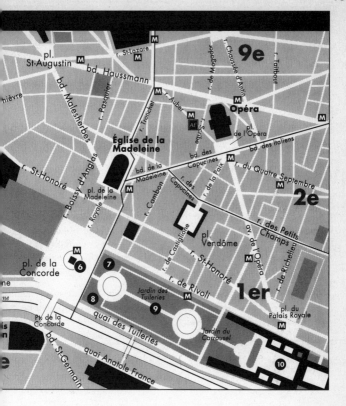

pl. St-Augustin

bd. Haussmann

r. St-Lazare

9e

r. Taitbout

r. de Mogador

r. Chaussée d'Antin

hièvre

bd. Malesherbes

r. Pasquier

r. Tronchet

r. Auber

Opéra

M

AE

pl. de l'Opéra

bd. des Italiens

Église de la Madeleine

bd. des Capucines

r. du Quatre Septembre

2e

r. St-Honoré

Boissy d'Anglas

bd. de la Madeleine

pl. de la Madeleine

r. Cambon

r. des Capucines

r. de la Paix

av. de l'Opéra

r. des Petits Champs

r. de Richelieu

r. Royale

r. de Castiglione

pl. Vendôme

r. St-Honoré

pl. de la Concorde

6

7

r. de Rivoli

1er

pl. du Palais Royale

8

Jardin des Tuileries

9

M

ne

Pt. de la Concorde

bd. St-Germain

quai des Tuileries

Jardin du Carrousel

is n

quai Anatole France

10

e

Foch, Paris's widest boulevard (120 yards across). The manifold attractions of Le Bois include cafés, restaurants, lakes, waterfalls, gardens, and museums. Rowboats can be rented at **Lac Inférieur** and **Lac Supérieur.** Meetings at **Longchamp** and **Auteuil** racetracks are high on the social calendar, as is the French Open tennis tournament at the beautiful **Roland Garros Stadium**, in late May. Buses traverse the Bois de Boulogne during the day (Service 244 from Porte Maillot), but Le Bois becomes a distinctly adult playground after dark, when prostitutes of various genders come prowling for clients. ⊠ *Main entrance at bottom of av. Foch. Métro: Porte Maillot, Porte Dauphine, Porte d'Auteuil; Bus 244.*

**Champs-Élysées.** The 2-km (1-mi) Champs-Élysées was originally laid out in the 1660s by the landscape gardener Le Nôtre as a garden sweeping away from the Tuileries. Explore both its commercial upper half and its verdant lower section. *Métro: George-V, Champs-Élysées–Clemenceau, Franklin-D.-Roosevelt.*

❷ **La Défense.** French planners, with their usual desire to rationalize, ordained that modern high-rise development be banished to the outskirts at La Défense, just west of Paris. The soaring skyscrapers are mainly taken up by offices, with no expense spared in the pursuit of visual ingenuity. The highlight is the giant **Grande Arche de La Défense**, aligned with avenue de la Grande-Armée, the Arc de Triomphe, the Champs-Élysées, and the Louvre. Tubular glass elevators whisk you to the top. ⊠ *Parvis de La Défense,* ☎ *01–49–07–27–57.* 🎟 *Arch 40 frs.* ☉ *Arch daily 10–7. Métro, RER: Grande Arche de La Défense.*

❺ **Grand Palais** (Grand Palace). With its curved glass roof, the Grand Palais is unmistakable when approached from either the Seine or the Champs-Élysées and forms an attractive duo with the **Petit Palais** on the other side of avenue Winston-Churchill. Both were built for the World's Fair of 1900, and, as with the Eiffel Tower, they were never intended to be permanent additions to the city. Unfortunately, the main hall of the Grand Palais has been closed for renovation since 1994, and its date of reopening is still unknown. But the Petit Palais contains a permanent collection of French painting and furniture, with splendid canvases by Courbet and Bouguereau. A statue of Winston Churchill was unveiled alongside the building by Queen Elizabeth II in 1998. ⊠ *av. Winston-Churchill,* ☎ *01–42–65–12–73.* 🎫 *27 frs.* ☉ *Tues.–Sun. 10–5:30. Métro: Champs-Élysées–Clemenceau.*

🐌 ❾ **Jardin des Tuileries** (Tuileries Garden). The Tuileries Garden is typically French: formal and neatly patterned, with rows of trees, gravel paths, flower beds, and a host of statues from varying eras. This is a delightful place to stroll and survey the surrounding cityscape. *Métro: Concorde, Tuileries.*

❿ **Louvre.** Though it's now a coherent, unified structure, the Louvre—the world's largest museum—is the product of centuries. Originally built by Philippe-Auguste in the 13th century as a fortress, it was not until the reign of pleasure-loving François I, 300 years later, that today's Louvre gradually began to take shape. Through the years Henri IV (1589–1610), Louis XIII (1610–43), Louis XIV (1643–1715), Napoléon (1804–14), and Napoléon III (1852–70) all contributed to its construction. The recent history of the Louvre centers on I. M. Pei's glass Pyramid, unveiled in March 1989, and numerous renovations. The number one attraction is Leonardo da Vinci's enigmatic *Mona Lisa* (*La Joconde,* to the French); be forewarned that you will find it encased in glass and surrounded by a mob of tourists. The collections are divided into seven sections: Asian antiquities; Egyptian antiquities; Greek and Roman antiquities; sculpture; paintings, prints, and drawings; furniture; and objets d'art. Don't try to see it all at once; try, instead, to make repeat visits—the admission is nearly half price on Sunday and after 3 PM on other days. (Unless you plan on going to a number of museums every day, the one-, three-, and five-day tourist museum passes probably aren't worth your money since you could easily spend a whole day at the Louvre alone.) Some other highlights of the paintings are *Shepherds in Arcadia,* by Nicolas Poussin (1594–1665); *The Oath of the Horatii,* by Jacques-Louis David (1748–1825); *The Raft of the Medusa,* by Théodore Géricault (1791–1824); and *La Grande Odalisque,* by Jean-Auguste-Dominique Ingres (1780–1867). The French crown jewels (in the objets d'art section of the Richelieu Wing) include the mind-boggling 186-carat Regent diamond. The *Winged*

*Victory of Samothrace* seems poised for flight at the top of
the stairs, and another much-loved piece of sculpture is
Michelangelo's pair of *Slaves*, intended for the tomb of Pope
Julius II. These can be admired in the Denon Wing, where
a new medieval and Renaissance sculpture section is housed
partly in the former imperial stables. In 1997 new rooms
for Persian, Arab, Greek, and Egyptian art were opened.
Come as early as possible to avoid the crowds. ⊠ *Palais
du Louvre (it's faster to enter through the Carrousel du Louvre mall on rue de Rivoli than through the pyramid),* ☎
*01–40–20–51–51.* 🎫 *45 frs; 26 frs after 3 PM and on Sun.;
free 1st Sun. of month.* ☉ *Thurs.–Sun. 9–6, Mon. and
Wed. 9 AM–9:45 PM. Some sections open limited days.
Métro: Palais-Royal.*

**❼ Musée du Jeu de Paume.** At the entrance to the Tuileries
Garden, this museum is an ultramodern white-walled show-
case for excellent temporary exhibits of bold contemporary
art. ⊠ *Pl. de la Concorde,* ☎ *01–42–60–69–69.* 🎫 *38 frs.*
☉ *Tues. noon–9:30, Wed.–Fri. noon–7, weekends 10–7.
Métro: Concorde.*

**❽ Musée de l'Orangerie.** Several of Claude Monet's *Water Lily*
series head the choice array of early 20th-century paintings
in this museum in the Tuileries Garden. ⊠ *Pl. de la Concorde,* ☎ *01–42–97–48–16.* 🎫 *30 frs.* ☉ *Wed.–Mon. 9:45–
5:15. Métro: Concorde.*

**❹ Office de Tourisme de la Ville de Paris** (Paris Tourist Office). The modern, spacious Paris Tourist Office, near the
Arc de Triomphe, is worth a visit at the start of your stay
to pick up free maps, leaflets, and information on upcoming events. Most of the staff speak English and can also help
book accommodations or tickets for shows. You can also
exchange money here and buy métro tickets and souvenirs.
⊠ *127 av. des Champs-Élysées,* ☎ *01–49–52–53–54 (01–
49–52–53–56 for recorded information in English).* ☉
*Daily 9–8. Métro: Charles-de-Gaulle–Étoile.*

**❻ Place de la Concorde.** This majestic square at the foot of the
Champs-Élysées was laid out in the 1770s, but there was
nothing in the way of peace or concord about its early years.
Between 1793 and 1795 more than a thousand victims, in-

cluding Louis XVI and Marie-Antoinette, were slashed into oblivion at the guillotine. The top of the 107-ft **Obelisk**—a present from the viceroy of Egypt in 1833—was regilded in 1998. *Métro: Concorde.*

## From the Eiffel Tower to Pont de l'Alma

The Eiffel Tower hovers over southwest Paris, and wherever you are on this walk, you can see it looming overhead. Water is the second theme: fountains playing beneath Place du Trocadéro and tours along the Seine on a Bateau Mouche. Museums are the third: The area around Trocadéro is full of them. And style is the fourth, but not just because the buildings here are overwhelmingly elegant—this is also the center of haute couture, with the top names in world fashion all congregated around avenue Montaigne, only a brief walk from the Champs-Élysées, to the north.

*Numbers in the margin correspond to numbers on the Eiffel Tower to Pont de l'Alma map; these numbers indicate a suggested path for sightseeing.*

### Sights to See

🕙 **❻ Bateaux Mouches.** These popular motorboats set off on their hour-long tours of Paris waters regularly (every half hour in summer). ⊠ *Pl. de l'Alma,* ☏ 01–40–76–99–99. 🎟 *40 frs. Métro: Alma-Marceau.*

🕙 **❶ Champ de Mars.** This long, formal garden, landscaped at the start of the century, lies between the Eiffel Tower and École Militaire. It was previously used as a parade ground and was the site of the World Exhibitions of 1867, 1889 (date of the construction of the Eiffel Tower), and 1900. *Métro: École Militaire; RER: Champ-de-Mars.*

**❺ Musée d'Art Moderne de la Ville de Paris** (City Museum of Modern Art). Both temporary exhibits and a permanent collection of top-quality 20th-century art can be found at this museum. It takes over, chronologically speaking, where the Musée d'Orsay (☞ From Orsay to St-Germain, *below*) leaves off: Among the earliest works are Fauve paintings by Vlaminck and Derain, followed by Picasso's early experiments in Cubism. Other highlights include works by

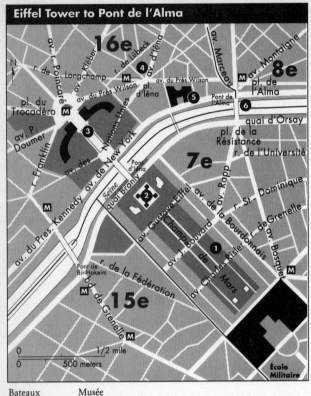

## Eiffel Tower to Pont de l'Alma

Bateaux Mouches, **6**

Champ de Mars, **1**

Musée d'Art Moderne de la Ville de Paris, **5**

Musée Guimet, **4**

Palais de Chaillot, **3**

Tour Eiffel, **2**

Braque, Rouault, Gleizes, Da Silva, Gromaire, and Modigliani. ⊠ *11 av. du Président-Wilson,* ☎ *01–53–67–40–00.* 🖃 *27 frs.* ☉ *Tues.–Fri. 10–5:30, weekends 10–6:45. Métro: Iéna.*

**❹ Musée Guimet.** This Belle Epoque museum was founded by Lyonnais industrialist Émile Guimet, who traveled around the world in the late 19th century amassing Indo-Chinese and Far Eastern objets d'art, plus a large collection of Cambodian art. After a massive renovation, the museum was due to reopen in early 2000. ⊠ *6 Pl. d'Iéna,* ☎ *01–45–05–00–98.* ☉ *Wed.–Mon. 9:45–6. Métro: Iéna.*

**❸ Palais de Chaillot** (Chaillot Palace). This honey-color, Art Deco culture center facing the Seine, perched atop tumbling gardens with sculpture and fountains, was built in the 1930s and houses three museums: the **Musée de l'Homme** (Museum of Mankind) with an array of prehistoric artifacts; the **Musée de la Marine** (Maritime Museum), with its salty collection of model ships, marine paintings, and naval paraphernalia; and the **Musée des Monuments Français** (Museum of French Monuments), damaged by fire in 1997 but due to reopen in 1999. ⊠ *Pl. du Trocadéro,* ☎ *Museum of Mankind 01–44–05–72–72; Maritime Museum 01–53–65–69–69; Museum of French Monuments 01–44–05–39–10.* 🖃 *Museum of Mankind 30 frs; Maritime Museum 38 frs.* ☉ *Museum of Mankind Wed.–Mon. 9:45–5:15; Maritime Museum Wed.–Mon. 10–6. Métro: Trocadéro.*

★ ⏱ **❷ Tour Eiffel** (Eiffel Tower). Known to the French as La Tour Eiffel (pronounced ef-*el*), Paris's most famous landmark was built by Gustave Eiffel for the World Exhibition of 1889, the centennial of the French Revolution, and was still in good shape to celebrate its own 100th birthday. Such was Eiffel's engineering wizardry that even in the strongest winds his tower never sways more than 4½ inches. If you're full of energy, stride up the stairs as far as the third deck. If you want to go to the top, you'll have to take the elevator. ⊠ *quai Branly,* ☎ *01–44–11–23–23.* 🖃 *By elevator: 2nd floor, 20 frs; 3rd floor, 42 frs; 4th floor, 59 frs. By foot: 2nd and 3rd floors only, 14 frs.* ☉ *July–Aug., daily 9 AM–midnight; Sept.–June, daily 9 AM–11 PM. Métro: Bir-Hakeim; RER: Champ-de-Mars.*

# The Faubourg St-Honoré

The Faubourg St-Honoré, north of the Champs-Élysées and the Tuileries, is synonymous with style—as you will see as you progress from the President's Palace, past a wealth of art galleries, to the monumental Madeleine church and on to stately Place Vendôme, home to the Ritz and the world's top jewelers. Leading names in modern fashion are found farther east on Place des Victoires, close to what was for centuries the gastronomic heart of Paris: Les Halles (pronounced lay-*ahl*), once the city's main market. In 1969 Les Halles was closed and replaced by a park and a modern shopping mall, the Forum des Halles. The brash modernity of the Forum stands in contrast to the August church of St-Eustache nearby. Similarly, the incongruous black-and-white columns in the classical courtyard of Richelieu's neighboring Palais-Royal present a further case of daring modernity—or architectural vandalism, depending on your point of view.

*Numbers in the margin correspond to numbers on the Faubourg St-Honoré map; these numbers indicate a suggested path for sightseeing.*

## Sights to See

**⑧ Bourse du Commerce** (Commercial Exchange). The 18th-century, circular, shallow-domed Commercial Exchange, near Les Halles, began life as a corn exchange; Victor Hugo waggishly likened it to a jockey's cap without the peak. ⊠ *rue de Viarmes. Métro or RER: Les Halles.*

**⑥ Comédie Française.** This theater is the setting for performances of classical French drama. The building itself dates from 1790, but the Comédie Française company was created by that most theatrical of French monarchs, Louis XIV, back in 1680. ⊠ *Pl. André-Malraux,* ☎ *01–44–58–15–15. Métro: Palais-Royal.*

**② Église de La Madeleine** (Church of La Madeleine). With its rows of uncompromising columns, this sturdy neoclassical edifice—designed in 1814 but not consecrated until 1842—looks more like a Greek temple than a Christian church. In fact, La Madeleine, as it is known, was nearly selected as Paris's first train station (the site of the Gare St-Lazare, just up the road, was chosen instead). Inside, the walls are richly and harmoniously decorated; gold glints through the murk. The portico's majestic Corinthian colonnade supports a gigantic pediment with a frieze of the Last Judgment. ⊠ *Pl. de la Madeleine.* ⊙ *Mon.–Sat. 7:30–7, Sun. 8–7. Métro: Madeleine.*

**⑪ Forum des Halles.** Les Halles, the iron-and-glass halls that made up the central Paris food market, were closed in 1969 and replaced in the late '70s by the Forum des Halles, a mundane shopping mall. Unfortunately, much of its plastic, concrete, glass, and mock-marble exterior is already showing signs of wear and tear. ⊠ *Main entrance on rue Pierre-Lescot. Métro: Les Halles; RER: Châtelet–Les Halles.*

---

NEED A BREAK?    Founded in 1903, **Angélina** (⊠ 226 rue de Rivoli, ☎ 01–42–60–82–00) is an elegant *salon de thé* (tearoom), famous for its hot chocolate so thick you'll need a fork to eat it (irresistible even in summer).

---

**⑤ Musée de la Mode** (Fashion Museum). This museum, housed in the northwestern wing of the Louvre building, has a glittering array of costumes and fashion accessories dating back to the 18th century. ⊠ *107 rue de Rivoli,* ☎ *01–44–55–57–50.* ⊡ *40 frs.* ⊙ *Tues.–Sun. 11–6. Métro: Palais-Royal.*

**❶ Palais de l'Élysée** (Élysée Palace). This "palace," known to the French simply as L'Élysée, where the French president lives, works, and receives official visitors, was originally constructed as a private mansion in 1718 and has housed presidents only since 1873. Although you can catch a glimpse of the palace forecourt and façade through the Faubourg St-Honoré gateway, it is difficult to get much idea of the building's size or of the extensive gardens that stretch back to the Champs-Élysées. ⊠ *55 rue du Faubourg–St-Honoré.* ⊙ *Not open to public. Métro: Miromesnil.*

**❼ Palais-Royal** (Royal Palace). The buildings of this former palace—royal only in that all-powerful Cardinal Richelieu (1585–1642) magnanimously bequeathed them to Louis XIII—date from the 1630s. Today the Palais-Royal is home to the French Ministry of Culture, and its buildings are not open to the public. You can, however, visit the colonnaded courtyard with black-and-white-stripe half columns and re-

# The Faubourg St-Honoré

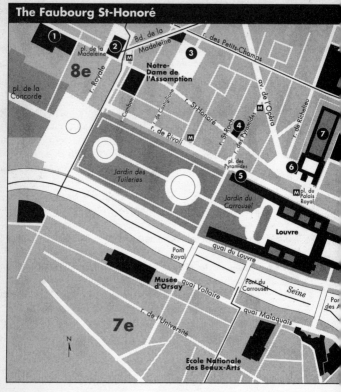

Bourse du
Commerce, **8**

Comédie
Française, **6**

Église de la
Madeleine, **2**

Forum des
Halles, **11**

Musée de la
Mode, **5**

Palais de
l'Elysée, **1**

Palais-Royal, **7**

Place
Vendôme, **3**

Place des
Victoires, **9**

St-Eustache, **10**

St-Germain
l'Auxerrois, **12**

St-Roch, **4**

r. Vivienne

r. N.-D. des Victoires

r. d'Aboukir

2e

220 yards
200 meters

r. Réaumur

M

M

9  Banque
   de France

r. Etienne Marcel

r. de Turbigo

7

10  pl.
    R. Cassin

M

bd. de Sébastopol

Pierre Lescot

r. St-Denis

3e

r. Beaubourg

M

8  1er

r. du Louvre

r. St-Honoré

11  M

r. Berger

r. Rambuteau

Centre Pompidou/
Beaubourg

Cr.aux des Petits-Champs

M

r. de Rivoli

Sq. des
Innocents

r. des Halles

r. St-Denis

M

M

M

12

r. de l'Amiral
de Coligny

r. de l'Arbre-Sec

r. de Pont Neuf

M

quai de la Mégisserie

r. St-Martin

r. de Rivoli

r. du Renard

4e

M

Pont
des Arts

Pont Neuf

Pont
au Change

M  pl. du
   Châtelet

pl. L.
Lépine

Pont
d'Arcole

volving silver spheres that slither around in two fountains—the controversial work of architect Daniel Buren—
and the more classical gardens beyond. ✉ *Pl. du
Palais-Royal. Métro: Palais-Royal.*

**❸ Place Vendôme.** Mansart's rhythmic, perfectly proportioned example of 17th-century urban architecture shines
in all its golden-stone splendor. The square is a fitting
showcase for the deluxe Ritz Hotel and the cluster of jewelry display windows found here. Napoléon had the square's
central column made from the melted bronze of 1,200 can-
nons captured at the Battle of Austerlitz in 1805. There he
is, perched vigilantly at the top. *Métro: Opéra.*

**❾ Place des Victoires.** This circular square, now home to
many of the city's top fashion boutiques, was laid out in
1685 by Jules-Hardouin Mansart in honor of the military
victories (*victoires*) of Louis XIV. The Sun King gallops along
on a bronze horse in the middle. *Métro: Sentier.*

**❿ St-Eustache.** A huge church, it was built as the people's Right
Bank reply to Notre-Dame, though St-Eustache dates from
a couple of hundred years later. The church is a curious architectural hybrid: With the exception of the feeble west
front, added between 1754 and 1788, construction lasted
from 1532 to 1637, spanning the decline of the Gothic style
and the emergence of the Renaissance. ✉ *2 rue du Jour,* ☎
*01–46–27–89–21 for concert information.* ☉ *Daily 8–7.*
*Métro: Les Halles; RER: Châtelet–Les Halles.*

**⓬ St-Germain l'Auxerrois.** Until 1789, in the days when the adjacent Louvre was a palace rather than a museum, St-Germain was used by the French royal family as its parish
church. The facade reveals the influence of 15th-century
Flamboyant Gothic style, while the fluted columns around
the choir, the area surrounding the altar, demonstrate the tri-
umph of Classicism. ✉ *Pl. du Louvre. Métro: Louvre-Rivoli.*

**❹ St-Roch.** Designed by Lemercier in 1653 but completed
only in the 1730s, this huge church is almost as long as
Notre-Dame (138 yards) thanks to Hardouin-Mansart's
domed Lady Chapel at the far end. ✉ *rue St-Honoré.*
*Métro: Tuileries.*

# The Grand Boulevards

An uninterrupted avenue runs in almost a straight line from St-Augustin, the city's grandest Second Empire church, to Place de la République, whose very name symbolizes the ultimate downfall of the imperial regime. The avenue's name changes six times along the way, which is why Parisians refer to it as the *Grands Boulevards* (plural). The makeup of the neighborhoods along the Grand Boulevards changes steadily as you head east from the posh $8^e$ arrondissement toward working-class east Paris. The *grands magasins* (department stores) at the start of the walk epitomize upscale Paris shopping. They stand on boulevard Haussmann, named in honor of the regional prefect who oversaw the reconstruction of the city in the 1850s and 1860s. The opulent Opéra Garnier, just past the *grands magasins,* is the architectural showpiece of the period (often termed the Second Empire and corresponding to the rule of Napoléon III).

*Numbers in the margin correspond to numbers on the Grand Boulevards map; these numbers indicate a suggested path for sightseeing.*

## Sights to See

❾ **Bourse** (Stock Exchange). The Paris Stock Exchange, a serene, colonnaded 19th-century building, is a far cry from Wall Street. Take your passport if you want to tour it. ⊠ *rue Vivienne.* 🎫 *30 frs.* ☉ *Guided tours only (in French), weekdays every ½ hr 1:15–3:45. Métro: Bourse.*

⑯ **Canal St-Martin.** The canal was built at the behest of Napoleon from 1802 to 1825, with the aim of providing the city with drinking water. It was not assigned to navigable traffic until the 1850s and was partly covered (between Bastille and République) by Haussmann in 1862. With its quiet banks, locks, and footbridges, the canal is much loved by novelists and film directors; Simenon's famous inspector Maigret solved many a mystery along its deceptively sleepy banks. Major development has transformed the northern end of the canal, around Place de Stalingrad and its 18th-century rotunda, and there are 10-franc boat trips (⊠ Embarkation at 13 quai de la Loire) along the once industrial Bassin de La Villette to the nearby Parc de La Villette. *Métro: Jacques-Bonsergent, Jaurès.*

# The Grand Boulevards

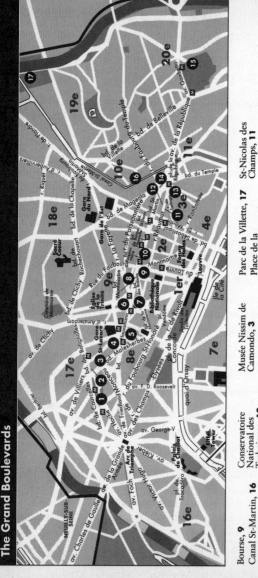

NEUILLY-SUR-SEINE

16e
17e
18e
19e
20e
10e
9e
8e
2e
1er
3e
4e
7e
11e

Arc de Triomphe
Sacré Coeur
Cimetière de Montmartre
Gare St-Lazare
Gare de l'Est
Gare du Nord
Église de la Trinité
Bibliothèque Nationale
Opéra
Montmartre
Forum des Halles
Île de la Cité

av. Charles de Gaulle
av. Foch
av. Kléber
av. Victor Hugo
av. Hoche
av. de Villiers
av. de Clichy
av. de Wagram
av. de Friedland
av. des Champs-Élysées
av. George-V
av. F. D. Roosevelt
quai d'Orsay
pl. du Trocadéro
Concorde
pl. Vendôme
bd. de Courcelles
bd. Malesherbes
bd. Haussmann
bd. des Batignolles
bd. de Clichy
bd. de Rochechouart
bd. de la Chapelle
bd. de Magenta
bd. Poissonnière
bd. Bonne Nouvelle
bd. St-Martin
bd. St-Denis
bd. du Temple
bd. de Belleville
bd. de la Villette
r. Riquet
r. d'Aubervilliers
r. de Flandre
r. du Faubourg St-Martin
r. du Faubourg Poissonnière
r. La Fayette
r. du Faubourg Montmartre
r. de Rivoli
r. du Faubourg St-Honoré
r. de Sébastopol
r. du Temple
Canal St-Martin
Canal St-Denis

Eiffel Tower
pl. de la République

Bourse, 9
Canal St-Martin, 16
Chapelle
Expiatoire, 5
Cimetière du Père
Lachaise, 15

Conservatoire
National des
Techniques, 12
Galeries Lafayette, 6
Hôtel Drouot, 8
Musée Cernuschi, 2

Musée Nissim de
Camondo, 3
Notre-Dame de
Bonne-Nouvelle, 10
Opéra Garnier, 7
Parc Monceau, 1

Parc de la Villette, 17
Place de la
République, 14
St-Augustin, 4
Ste-Élisabeth, 13

St-Nicolas des
Champs, 11

**⑤ Chapelle Expiatoire.** This unkempt mausoleum emerges defiantly from the lush undergrowth of verdant square Louis-XVI off boulevard Haussmann, marking the initial burial site of Louis XVI and Marie-Antoinette after their turns at the guillotine on Place de la Concorde. Two stone tablets are inscribed with the last missives of the doomed royals: touching pleas for their Revolutionary enemies to be forgiven. ⌧ *29 rue Pasquier*, ☎ *01–44–32–18–00.* ▧ *15 frs.* ☼ *Thurs.–Sat. 1–5. Métro: St-Augustin.*

**⑮ Cimetière du Père Lachaise** (Father Lachaise Cemetery). Cemeteries may not be your idea of the ultimate attraction, but this is the largest and most interesting in Paris. It forms a veritable necropolis, with cobbled avenues and tombs competing in pomposity and originality. Leading incumbents include Jim Morrison, Frédéric Chopin, Marcel Proust, Edith Piaf, and Gertrude Stein. Get a map at the entrance and track them down. ⌧ *Entrances on rue des Rondeaux, bd. de Ménilmontant, rue de la Réunion.* ☼ *Apr.–Sept., daily 8–6, Oct.–Mar., daily 8–5. Métro: Gambetta, Philippe-Auguste, Père Lachaise.*

**⑫ Conservatoire National des Techniques** (National Technical Museum). The former church and priory of St-Martin des Champs was built between the 11th and 13th centuries. Confiscated during the Revolution, it was used first as an educational institution, then as an arms factory, before becoming, in 1799, the Conservatoire des Arts et Métiers. Today the church forms the south wing of the National Technical Museum, an industrial museum with a varied collection of models (locomotives, vehicles, and agricultural machinery), astronomical instruments, looms, and glass, together with displays on printing, photography, and the history of television. The splendid 13th-century refectory, a large hall supported by central columns, is now used as a library. The museum was set to reopen in late 1999 after major renovations. ⌧ *292 rue St-Martin,* ☎ *01–40–27–23–31. Métro: Arts et Métiers.*

**⑥ Galeries Lafayette.** This turn-of-the-century department store has a vast, shimmering, Belle Epoque glass dome that can only be seen if you venture inside (☞ Chapter 7). ⌧ *40 bd. Haussmann. Métro: Chaussée d'Antin; RER: Auber.*

**⑧ Hôtel Drouot.** Paris's central auction house has everything from stamps and toy soldiers to Renoirs and 18th-century commodes. The 16 salesrooms make for fascinating browsing, and there's no obligation to bid. ✉ *9 rue Drouot,* ☎ *01–48–00–20–00.* ⊙ *Viewings Mon.–Sat. 11–noon and 2–6, with auctions starting at 2. Closed mid-July–mid-Sept. Métro: Richelieu-Drouot.*

**② Musée Cernuschi.** The collection includes Chinese art from Neolithic pottery (3rd century BC) to funeral statuary, painted 8th-century silks, and contemporary paintings, as well as ancient Persian bronze objects. ✉ *7 av. Velasquez,* ☎ *01–45–63–50–75.* ▦ *17 frs.* ⊙ *Tues.–Sun. 10–5:40. Métro: Monceau.*

**③ Musée Nissim de Camondo.** The elegant decadence of the last days of the regal Ancien Régime is fully reflected in the lavish interior of this aristocratic Parisian mansion, built in the style of Louis XVI. ✉ *63 rue de Monceau,* ☎ *01–53–89–06–40.* ▦ *27 frs.* ⊙ *Wed.–Sun. 10–5. Métro: Monceau.*

**⑩ Notre-Dame de Bonne-Nouvelle.** This wide, soberly Neoclassical church, built 1823–29, is tucked away off the Grand Boulevards. ✉ *rue de la Lune. Métro: Bonne-Nouvelle.*

**⑦ Opéra Garnier.** The original Paris Opera, begun in 1862 by Charles Garnier at the behest of Napoléon III, was not completed until 1875, five years after the emperor's abdication. The ornate facade, cleaned 1999–2000, typifies Second Empire architecture: a pompous hodgepodge of styles, with all the subtlety of a Wagnerian cymbal crash. After paying the entrance fee, you can stroll around at leisure. The monumental foyer and staircase are impressive, and the stage is the largest in the world. Marc Chagall painted the ceiling in 1964. The **Musée de l'Opéra**, containing a few paintings and theatrical mementos, is unremarkable. ✉ *Pl. de l'Opéra,* ☎ *01–40–01–22–63.* ▦ *30 frs, guided tours in English at 3 PM, 60 frs.* ⊙ *Daily 10–5:30; closed occasionally for rehearsals; call 01–47–42–57–50 to check. Métro: Opéra.*

---

NEED A
BREAK?

Few cafés in Paris are grander than the Belle Epoque **Café de la Paix** (✉ 5 Pl. de l'Opéra, ☎ 01–40–07–30–10).

⚐ **❶ Parc Monceau.** The most picturesque gardens on the Right Bank were laid out as a private park in 1778 and retain some of the fanciful elements then in vogue, including mock ruins and a phony pyramid. ⊠ *Entrances on bd. de Courcelles, av. Velasquez, av. Ruysdaël, av. van Dyck. Métro: Monceau.*

★ ⚐ **❶⃝ Parc de La Villette.** Until the 1970s when it was transformed into an ambitiously landscaped, futuristic park, this 130-acre site was home to a cattle market and *abattoir* (slaughterhouse). Known as La Villette, it has sweeping lawns, a children's playground, canopied walkways, a cinema, two museums, brightly painted pavilions, and a state-of-the-art concert hall, the **Cité de la Musique** (☞ Chapter 5). This giant postmodern musical academy also houses the outstanding **Musée de la Musique** (Museum of Musical Instruments). The former slaughterhouse—the **Grande Halle**—is a magnificent structure whose transformation into an arts center provides an intelligent link with the site's historic past. At the **Géode** cinema, which looks like a huge silver golf ball, films are shown on an enormous 180-degree-curved screen. The science museum, the **Cité des Sciences et de l'Industrie**, contains dozens of interactive exhibits (though most displays are in French only). ⊠ *Science Museum 30 av. Corentin-Cariou,* ☎ *Science Museum 01–40–05–80–00.* ▦ *Museum of Musical Instruments 35 frs; Science Museum 35 frs.* ☾ *Museum of Musical Instruments: Tues.–Sun. noon–6; Science Museum: Tues.–Sun. 10–6. Métro: Porte de La Villette, Porte de Pantin.*

**❶⃝ Place de la République.** This large, oblong square, laid out by Haussmann in 1856–65, is dominated by a matronly, Stalin-size statue symbolizing *The Republic* (1883). The square is often used as a rallying point for demonstrations. *Métro: République.*

**❹ St-Augustin.** This domed church was dexterously constructed in the 1860s within the confines of an awkward V-shape site. It represented a breakthrough in ecclesiastical engineering because the use of metal pillars and girders obviated the need for exterior buttressing. ⊠ *Pl. St-Augustin. Métro: St-Augustin.*

⑬ **Ste-Élisabeth.** This studied essay in Baroque (1628–46) has brightly restored wall paintings and a wide, semicircular apse around the choir. ⊠ *rue du Temple. Métro: Temple.*

⑪ **St-Nicolas des Champs.** The rounded-arch, fluted Doric capitals in the chancel of this church date from 1560 to 1587, a full century later than the pointed-arch nave (1420–80). ⊠ *rue St-Martin. Métro: Arts-et-Métiers.*

---

## The Marais and the Bastille

The Marais is one of the city's most historic and sought-after residential districts. Except for the architecturally whimsical Pompidou Center, the tone here is set by the gracious architecture of the 17th and 18th centuries (the Marais was spared the attentions of Haussmann, the man who rebuilt so much of Paris in the mid-19th century). Today most of the Marais's spectacular *hôtels particuliers*—loosely translated as "mansions," the onetime residences of aristocratic families—have been restored; many are now museums. There are trendy boutiques and cafés among the kosher shops in what used to be a predominantly Jewish neighborhood around rue des Rosiers, and there's an impressive new Jewish Museum on nearby rue du Temple.

On the eastern edge of the Marais is Place de la Bastille, site of the infamous prison stormed on July 14, 1789, an event that came to symbolize the beginning of the French Revolution. Largely in commemoration of the bicentennial of the revolution, the Bastille area was renovated and became one of the trendiest sections of Paris. Galleries, shops, theaters, cafés, restaurants, and bars now fill formerly decrepit buildings and alleys.

*Numbers in the margin correspond to numbers on the Marais and the Bastille map; these numbers indicate a suggested path for sightseeing.*

### Sights to See

⑬ **Archives Nationales** (National Archives). If you're a serious history buff, you'll be fascinated by the thousands of intricate historical documents, dating from the Merovingian period to the 20th century, at the National Archives.

⊠ *60 rue des Francs-Bourgeois,* ☎ *01–40–27–62–18.* 🎟 *20 frs.* ☉ *Wed.–Mon. 1:45–5:45. Métro: Rambuteau.*

**⑩ Atelier Brancusi** (Brancusi Studio). Romanian-born sculptor Constantin Brancusi settled in Paris in 1898 at age 22. This light, airy museum in front of the Pompidou Center contains four glass-fronted rooms that re-create Brancusi's studio, crammed with smooth, stylized works from all periods of his career. ⊠ *11 rue St-Paul,* ☎ *01–44–78–12–33.* 🎟 *20 frs.* ☉ *Wed.–Mon. noon–10. Métro: Rambuteau.*

**⑪ Centre Pompidou.** The futuristic, funnel-top Pompidou Center—known to Parisians as Beaubourg, after the surrounding district—was built in the mid-1970s and named in honor of former French president Georges Pompidou (1911–74). After receiving many more visitors than intended over the years, the center was closed in 1996 for top-to-bottom renovation; it is to reopen on the eve of 2000. You approach the center across **Place Georges-Pompidou,** a sloping piazza, home to the **Atelier Brancusi** (☞ *above*). The center is most famous for its **Musée National d'Art Moderne** (Modern Art Museum). The emphasis here is largely on French works, from Fauvism and Cubism to postwar abstract art. Also look for rotating exhibits of contemporary art. In addition, there's a public reference library, a language laboratory, an industrial design center, a cinema, a café, a restaurant, and a gift shop. ⊠ *Pl. Georges-Pompidou,* ☎ *01–44–78–12–33.* 🎟 *Admission prices were unavailable at press time.* ☉ *Wed.–Mon. noon–10. Métro: Rambuteau, Châtelet–Les Halles, Hôtel de Ville.*

**③ Hôtel de Sully.** This late-Renaissance mansion, begun in 1624, has a stately garden and a majestic courtyard with statues, richly carved pediments, and dormer windows. It is the headquarters of the **Caisse Nationale des Monuments Historiques** (National Treasury of Historic Monuments), responsible for administering France's historic monuments. Guided visits to Paris sites and buildings begin here, though all are conducted in French. ⊠ *62 rue St-Antoine,* ☎ *01–44–61–20–00. Métro: St-Paul.*

**⑧ Hôtel de Ville** (City Hall). During the Commune of 1871, the Hôtel de Ville was burned to the ground. Today's building, based closely on the 16th-century Renaissance origi-

## The Marais and the Bastille

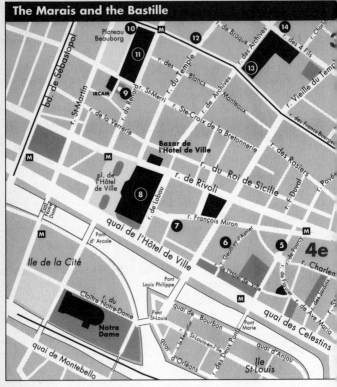

Archives Nationales, **13**

Atelier Brancusi, **10**

Centre Pompidou, **11**

Hôtel de Sully, **3**

Hôtel de Ville, **8**

Maison Européenne de la Photographie, **5**

Mémorial du Martyr Inconnu, **6**

Musée d'Art et d'Histoire du Judaïsme, **12**

Musée Bricard, **15**

Musée Carnavalet, **18**

Musée de la Chasse et de la Nature, **14**

Musée Cognacq-Jay, **17**

Musée Picasso, **16**

Opéra de la Bastille, **2**

Place de la Bastille, **1**

Place des Vosges, **19**

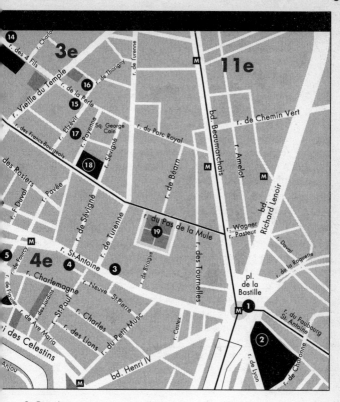

St-Gervais–
St-Protais, **7**

St-Paul–
St-Louis, **4**

Square Igor-
Stravinsky, **9**

nal, went up between 1874 and 1884. You can't inspect the lavish interior, but head around left to the traffic-free square, with its fountains and forest of street lamps, to admire the exuberant facade. ✉ *Pl. de l'Hôtel-de-Ville. Métro: Hôtel-de-Ville.*

**⑤ Maison Européenne de la Photographie** (European Photography Center). This museum, unveiled in 1996, combines spacious modern galleries with the original stonework of a venerable hôtel particulier. Despite its name, the museum has an impressive collection of both European and American photography, and stages up to four different exhibitions every three months. ✉ *5 rue Fourcy,* ☎ *01–44–78–75–00.* ✆ *30 frs. Free Wed. after 5 PM.* ☉ *Wed.–Sun. 11–8. Métro: St-Paul.*

**⑥ Mémorial du Martyr Inconnu** (Memorial of the Unknown Martyr). In March 1992, this memorial was erected at the **Center for Contemporary Jewish Documentation**—50 years after the first French Jews were deported from France—to honor the memory of the 6 million Jews who died "without graves" at the hands of the Nazis. The basement crypt has a dramatic, black marble Star of David containing the ashes of victims from Nazi death camps in Poland and Austria. The center has archives, a library, and a gallery that hosts temporary exhibitions. ✉ *17 rue Geoffroy-l'Asnier,* ☎ *01–42–77–44–72.* ✆ *15 frs.* ☉ *Sun.–Fri. 10–1 and 2–5:30. Métro: Pont-Marie.*

**⑫ Musée d'Art et d'Histoire du Judaïsme** (Museum of Jewish Art and History). With its clifflike courtyard ringed by giant pilasters, Pierre Le Muet's Hôtel St-Aignan—completed 1650—is one of the most awesome sights in the Marais. It opened as a museum in 1998 after a 20-year, $35 million restoration. The interior has been remodeled to the point of blandness, but the displays—including silverware, clothing, and furniture—are carefully lighted, with an array of explanatory English texts on Jewish history and ceremonies. Highlights include 13th-century tombstones excavated in Paris; wooden models of destroyed East European synagogues; a roomful of early Chagalls; and Christian Boltanksi's stark memorial to Shoah victims. ✉ *71 rue du Temple,* ☎ *01–53–01–86–53.* ✆ *40 frs.* ☉ *Sun.–Fri. 11–6. Métro: Rambuteau.*

🕐 ⓫ **Musée Bricard.** This museum—also called the Musée de la Serrure (Lock Museum)—is housed in a sober Baroque mansion designed in 1685 by the architect of Les Invalides, Libéral Bruand, for himself. If you've got a taste for fine craftsmanship, you will appreciate the intricacy and ingenuity of many of the locks displayed here. ⊠ *1 rue de la Perle,* ☎ *01–42–77–79–62.* 🎟 *30 frs.* ☉ *Weekdays 2–5. Métro: St-Paul.*

⓰ **Musée Carnavalet.** Two adjacent mansions in the heart of the Marais house the Carnavalet Museum, or the Paris History Museum, with material dating from the city's origins to the present. The museum is full of maps and plans, furniture, and busts and portraits of Parisian worthies down the ages. ⊠ *23 rue de Sévigné,* ☎ *01–42–72–21–13.* 🎟 *27 frs.* ☉ *Tues.–Sun. 10–5:30. Métro: St-Paul.*

NEED A BREAK?    **Marais Plus** (⊠ 20 rue des Francs-Bourgeois, ☎ 01–48–87–01–40), on the corner of rue Elzévir and rue des Francs-Bourgeois, is a delightful, artsy gift shop with a cozy *salon de thé* at the rear.

⓮ **Musée de la Chasse et de la Nature** (Museum of Hunting and Nature). This museum is housed in the Hôtel de Guénégaud, designed around 1650 by François Mansart. There is a series of immense 17th- and 18th-century still lifes (notably by Desportes and Oudry) and a wide variety of swords, guns, muskets, and taxidermy. ⊠ *60 rue des Archives,* ☎ *01–42–72–86–42.* 🎟 *30 frs.* ☉ *Wed.–Mon. 10–12:30 and 1:30–5:30. Métro: Rambuteau.*

⓱ **Musée Cognacq-Jay.** This museum, devoted to the arts of the 18th century, contains outstanding furniture, porcelain, and paintings (notably by Watteau, Boucher, and Tiepolo). ⊠ *8 rue Elzévir,* ☎ *01–40–27–07–21.* 🎟 *17 frs.* ☉ *Tues.–Sun. 10–5:40. Métro: St-Paul.*

⓰ **Musée Picasso.** Housed in the 17th-century Hôtel Salé, this museum contains the paintings, sculptures, drawings, prints, ceramics, and assorted works of art given to the government by Picasso's heirs after the painter's death in 1973 in lieu of death duties. There are works from every period of Picasso's life, as well as pieces by Cézanne, Miró, Renoir, Braque, Degas, and Matisse. ⊠ *5 rue de Thorigny,* ☎ *01–*

*42–71–25–21.* ✉ *30 frs, Sun. 20 frs.* ☉ *Wed.–Mon. 9:30–5:30. Métro: St-Sébastien.*

**②  Opéra de la Bastille.** The state-of-the-art Bastille Opera was erected on the south side of Place de la Bastille. Designed by Argentine-born Carlos Ott, it opened on July 14, 1989, in commemoration of the bicentennial of the French Revolution. The steep-climbing auditorium seats more than 3,000 and has earned more plaudits than the curving glass facade. ✉ *Pl. de la Bastille,* ☎ *01–44–73–13–00.* ✉ *Guided tours 50 frs. Métro: Bastille.*

**①  Place de la Bastille.** Nothing remains of the infamous Bastille prison destroyed at the beginning of the French Revolution. In the midst of the large traffic circle is the **Colonne de Juillet** (July Column), commemorating the overthrow of Charles X in July 1830. As part of the countrywide celebrations for July 1989, the bicentennial of the French Revolution, the Opéra de la Bastille (☞ *above*) was erected, inspiring substantial redevelopment on the surrounding streets, especially along rue de Lappe and rue de la Roquette. What was formerly a humdrum neighborhood rapidly gained art galleries, clubs, and bars. *Métro: Bastille.*

**⑲  Place des Vosges.** Laid out by Henri IV at the start of the 17th century and originally known as Place Royale, this square is the oldest and one of the prettiest in Paris. The two larger buildings on either side were originally the king's and queen's pavilions. The statue in the center is of Louis XIII. At No. 6 is the **Maison de Victor Hugo** (Victor Hugo House), where the workaholic French author, famed for *Les Misérables* and *The Hunchback of Notre-Dame,* lived between 1832 and 1848. ✉ *Maison de Victor Hugo: 6 Pl. des Vosges,* ☎ *01–42–72–10–16.* ✉ *27 frs.* ☉ *Tues.–Sun. 10–5:45. Métro: St-Paul, Chemin-Vert.*

**⑦  St-Gervais–St-Protais.** This imposing church near the Hôtel de Ville is named after two Roman soldiers martyred by the emperor Nero in the 1st century AD. The church, a riot of Flamboyant style, went up between 1494 and 1598, making it one of the last Gothic constructions in the country. The facade, constructed between 1616 and 1621, is an early example of French use of classical decoration on the capitals (topmost sections) of the columns. ✉ *Pl. St-Ger-*

*vais,* ☎ *01–47–26–78–38 for concert information.* ☉ *Tues.– Sun. 6:30 AM–8 PM. Métro: Hôtel-de-Ville.*

**❹ St-Paul–St-Louis.** The leading Baroque church in the Marais, with its elegant dome soaring 180 ft above the crossing, was begun in 1627 by the Jesuits and partly modeled on their Gesu church in Rome. Look for Delacroix's dramatic *Christ on the Mount of Olives* high up in the transept. ✉ *rue St-Antoine. Métro: St-Paul.*

**❾ Square Igor-Stravinsky.** The café-lined square, next to the Pompidou Center and backed by the church of St-Merri, has a fountain animated by the colorful and imaginative sculptures of French artist Niki de St-Phalle, together with the aquatic mechanisms of her Swiss partner Jean Tinguely. The fountain (sculptures and all) was erected in 1980. It is not part of the Pompidou Center, but it fits right in. *Métro: Rambuteau.*

## The Islands and the Latin Quarter

Of the two islands in the Seine—the Ile St-Louis and the Ile de la Cité—it is the Ile de la Cité that forms the historic heart of Paris. It was here that the earliest inhabitants of Paris, the Gaulish tribe of the Parisii, settled in about 250 BC. They called their little home Lutetia, meaning "settlement surrounded by water." Although the Ile St-Louis is today largely residential, the Ile de la Cité remains deeply historic. It has been inhabited for more than 2,000 years and is the site of the great, brooding cathedral of Notre-Dame. Most of the island's other medieval buildings fell victim to Haussmann's ambitious rebuilding in the 1860s. Among the rare survivors are the jewel-like Ste-Chapelle, a vision of shimmering stained glass, and the Conciergerie, the former city prison.

South of Ile de la Cité on the Left Bank of the Seine is the bohemian Quartier Latin (Latin Quarter), with its warren of steep, sloping streets, populated largely by Sorbonne students and academics. The name *Latin Quarter* comes from the old university tradition of studying and speaking in Latin, a tradition that disappeared during the Revolution. The university began as a theological school in the Middle Ages and later became the headquarters of the University of

Paris; in 1968 the student revolution here had an explosive effect on French politics, resulting in major reforms in the education system. Most of the district's appeal is less emphatic: Roman ruins, tumbling street markets, the two oldest trees in Paris, and chance glimpses of Notre-Dame all await your discovery.

*Numbers in the margin correspond to numbers on the Islands and the Latin Quarter map; these numbers indicate a suggested path for sightseeing.*

## Sights to See

🖐 ⑯ **Arènes de Lutèce** (Lutèce Arena). This Roman arena was only discovered in 1869 and has since been excavated and landscaped to reveal parts of the original amphitheater. Designed as a theater and circus, the arena was almost totally destroyed by the Barbarians in AD 280, although you can still see part of the stage and tiered seating. ✉ *Entrances on rue Monge and rue de Navarre.* ☉ *Daily 8–sunset. Métro: Monge.*

⑮ **Bibliothèque François-Mitterrand** (National Library). The last of former president Mitterrand's *grands travaux* (great building projects) opened in early 1997. The new library subsumes the majority of the collections in the old Bibliothèque Nationale on rue Richelieu and, with some 11 million volumes between its walls, surpasses the Library of Congress as the largest library in the world. Architect Dominique Perrault's controversial design features four soaring 24-story towers. A stunning interior courtyard—sunk beneath ground level, with its thicket of mighty evergreens invisible as you approach—provides breathing space. You can visit part of the library for free or pay 20 francs to consult more than 300,000 books. ✉ *11 quai François-Mauriac,* ☎ *01–53–79–59–59.* ☉ *Mid-Sept.–Aug., Tues.–Sat. 10–7, Sun. noon–6. Métro: Bibliothèque.*

❷ **Conciergerie.** This turreted medieval building by the Seine was originally part of the royal palace on Ile de la Cité. Most people know it, however, as the prison whence Danton, Robespierre, and Marie-Antoinette were bundled off to the guillotine. You can visit Marie-Antoinette's cell, the guardroom, and the monumental Salle des Gens d'Armes (Hall of the Men-at-Arms). ✉ *1 quai de l'Horloge,* ☎ *01–53–73–78–*

# The Islands and the Latin Quarter

Arènes de Lutèce, **16**

Bibliothèque François-Mitterrand, **15**

Conciergerie, **2**

Grande Galerie de l'Evolution, **14**

Ile St-Louis, **18**

Institut du Monde Arabe, **17**

Jardin des Plantes, **13**

Mémorial de la Déportation, **20**

Mosquée, **12**

Musée National du Moyen-Age, **8**

Notre-Dame, **5**

Palais de Justice, **3**

Panthéon, **11**

Pont de l'Arche-vêché, **21**

Pont Neuf, **1**

Ste-Chapelle, **4**

St-Étienne-du-Mont, **10**

St-Julien-le-Pauvre, **6**

St-Louis-en-l'Ile, **19**

St-Séverin, **7**

Sorbonne, **9**

50. ⛶ 32 frs; joint ticket with Ste-Chapelle 50 frs. ☉ Spring–
fall, daily 9:30–6:30; winter, daily 10–5. Métro: Cité.

🖐 **⑭** **Grande Galerie de l'Evolution** (Great Hall of Evolution).
This vast, handsome glass-and-iron structure in the Jardin
des Plantes was built, like the Eiffel Tower, in 1889, but
unlike the tower, it was abandoned in the 1960s. It now
contains one of the world's finest collections of taxidermy,
including a section devoted to extinct and endangered
species. ⊠ 36 rue Geoffroy-St-Hilaire, ☎ 01–40–79–39–
39. ⛶ 40 frs. ☉ Wed. and Fri.–Mon. 10–6, Thurs. 10–10.
Métro: Monge.

**⑱** **Ile St-Louis.** The smaller of the two Paris islands displays
striking architectural unity, which stems from the efforts
of a group of early 17th-century property speculators led
by Christophe Marie. The group commissioned leading
Baroque architect Louis Le Vau (1612–70) to erect a series
of imposing town houses. Métro: Pont-Marie.

. . . . . . . . . . . . . . . . . . . . . . . . . . . . . . . . . . . . . . . . . . . . . . . . . . . . . . . . . . . . . . . . . . . . . . . . . . .

NEED A        Cafés all over sell Berthillon, the haute couture of ice cream,
BREAK?        but the **Berthillon** (⊠ 31 rue St-Louis-en-l'Ile, ☎ 01–43–54–
              31–61) shop itself is the place to come. More than 30 fla-
              vors are served; expect to wait in line. The shop is open
              Wednesday–Sunday.

. . . . . . . . . . . . . . . . . . . . . . . . . . . . . . . . . . . . . . . . . . . . . . . . . . . . . . . . . . . . . . . . . . . . . . . . . . .

**⑰** **Institut du Monde Arabe** (Arab World Institute). Jean Nouvel's striking 1988 glass-and-steel edifice adroitly fuses
Arabic and European styles. Note the 240 shutterlike aper-
tures that open and close to regulate light exposure. Inside,
the institute tries to do for Arab culture what the Pompidou Center does for modern art, with the help of a sound-
and-image center, a vast library and documentation center,
and an art museum. The top-floor café provides a good view
of Paris. ⊠ 1 rue des Fossés-St-Bernard, ☎ 01–40–51–38–
38. ⛶ 40 frs. ☉ Tues.–Sun. 10–6. Métro: Cardinal-Lemoine.

🖐 **⑬** **Jardin des Plantes** (Botanical Garden). This enormous
swath of greenery contains the botanical garden, the Grande
Galerie de l'Évolution (☞ above), and three natural history
museums: the **Musée Entomologique** (15-franc admission),
devoted to insects; the **Musée Paléontologique** (30-franc admission), to fossils and prehistoric animals; and the **Musée
Minéralogique** (30-franc admission), to rocks and miner-

als. It also has an alpine garden, an aquarium, a maze, a number of hothouses, and one of the world's oldest zoos. ⊠ *Entrances on rue Geoffroy-St-Hilaire, rue Cuvier and rue Buffon.* 🎟 *Zoo 30 frs.* ⊙ *Garden daily 7:30–sunset; zoo: daily 9–6; museums: Wed.–Mon. 10–5. Métro: Monge, Jussieu, Gare d'Austerlitz.*

**㉜ Mémorial de la Déportation** (Deportation Memorial). On the eastern tip of the Ile de la Cité, in what was once the city morgue, lies a starkly moving modern crypt, dedicated to those French men, women, and children who died in Nazi concentration camps. 🎟 *Free.* ⊙ *Spring–fall, daily 9–6; winter, daily 9–dusk. Métro: Maubert-Mutualité.*

**⑫ Mosquée** (Mosque). The city mosque was built from 1922 to 1925, complete with arcades and minaret, and decorated in the style of Moorish Spain. The sunken garden and tiled patios are open to the public (the prayer rooms are not) and so are the *hammams,* or Turkish baths. Venture in and sip a restorative cup of sweet mint tea at the café. ⊠ *2 Pl. du Puits-de-l'Ermite,* ☎ *01–45–35–97–33.* 🎟 *15 frs guided tour, 85 frs Turkish baths.* ⊙ *Baths daily 10 AM–9 PM; Tues. and Sun. men only; Mon. and Wed.–Sat. women only. Guided tours of mosque Sat.–Thurs. 10–noon and 2–6. Métro: Monge.*

**⑧ Musée National du Moyen-Age** (National Museum of the Middle Ages). This museum is housed in the 15th-century Hôtel de Cluny. The mansion has an intricately vaulted chapel and a cloistered courtyard with mullioned windows that originally belonged to monks of the Cluny Abbey in Burgundy, hence the museum's former name, the Musée de Cluny. A stunning array of tapestries heads its vast exhibition of medieval decorative arts. Alongside the mansion are the city's Roman baths and the *Boatmen's Pillar,* Paris's oldest sculpture. ⊠ *6 Pl. Paul-Painlevé,* ☎ *01–53–73–78–00.* 🎟 *30 frs, Sun. 20 frs.* ⊙ *Wed.–Mon. 9:15–5:45. Métro: Cluny–La Sorbonne.*

★ **⑤ Notre-Dame.** Looming above the large, pedestrian Place du Parvis is Notre-Dame Cathedral, the most enduring symbol of Paris. Begun in 1163, it was not completed until 1345. The facade seems perfectly proportioned until you notice that the north (left) tower is wider than the south tower.

The south tower houses the great bell of Notre-Dame, as tolled by Quasimodo, Victor Hugo's fictional hunchback. The cathedral interior, with its vast proportions, soaring nave, and soft multicolor light filtering through the stained-glass windows, inspires awe despite the inevitable throngs of tourists. Visit early in the morning, when the cathedral is at its lightest and least crowded. Window space is limited and filled with shimmering stained glass; the circular rose windows in the transept are particularly delicate. The 387-step climb up the towers is worth the effort for a perfect view of the famous gargoyles and the heart of Paris. ⊠ *Pl. du Parvis.* 🎫 *Towers 32 frs.* ☉ *Cathedral 8 AM–7 PM; towers summer, daily 9:30–7:30; winter, daily 10–5. Métro: Cité.*

**❸ Palais de Justice** (Law Courts). In about 1860 the city law courts were built by Baron Haussmann in his characteristically weighty Neoclassical style. You can wander around the buildings, watch the bustle of the lawyers, or attend a court hearing. But the real interest here is the medieval part of the complex, spared by Haussmann: Conciergerie and Ste-Chapelle (☞ *above* and *below,* respectively). ⊠ *bd. du Palais. Métro: Cité.*

**⓫ Panthéon.** Originally commissioned as a church by Louis XV as a mark of gratitude for his recovery from a grave illness in 1744, the Panthéon is now a monument to France's most glorious historical figures, including Voltaire, Zola, Rousseau, and dozens of French statesmen, military heroes, and other thinkers. Germain Soufflot's building was not begun until 1764 and not completed until 1790, during the French Revolution, whereupon its windows were blocked and it was transformed into the national shrine it is today. A giant pendulum, suspended on a 220-ft steel wire, commemorates Léon Foucault's 1851 experiment to prove the earth's rotation. ⊠ *Pl. du Panthéon,* ☎ *01–44–32–18–00.* 🎫 *32 frs.* ☉ *Summer, daily 9:30–6:30; winter, daily 10–6:15. Métro: Cardinal-Lemoine; RER: Luxembourg.*

**㉑ Pont de l'Archevêché** (Archbishop's Bridge). This bridge, built in 1828, links Ile St-Louis to the Left Bank. The bridge offers a breathtaking view of the east end of the cathedral, ringed by flying buttresses, floating above the Seine like some vast stone ship. *Métro: Maubert-Mutualité.*

**❶ Pont Neuf** (New Bridge). Crossing the Ile de la Cité, just behind Square du Vert-Galant, is the oldest bridge in Paris, confusingly called the New Bridge, or Pont Neuf. It was completed in 1607 and was the first bridge in the city to be built without houses lining either side. *Métro: Pont-Neuf.*

★ **❹ Ste-Chapelle** (Holy Chapel). This chapel was built by Louis IX (1226–70), later canonized St. Louis, in the 1240s to house what he believed to be Christ's Crown of Thorns, purchased from Emperor Baldwin of Constantinople. The building's lead-covered wood spire, rebuilt in 1854, rises 246 ft. The somewhat garish lower chapel is less impressive than the upper one, whose walls consist of little else but dazzling 13th-century stained glass. ✉ *4 bd. du Palais,* ☎ *01–43–54–30–09 for concert information.* 🎫 *32 frs; joint ticket with Conciergerie 50 frs.* ☼ *Apr.–Sept., daily 9:30–6:30; Oct.–Mar., daily 10–5. Métro: Cité.*

**❿ St-Etienne-du-Mont.** The ornate facade of this mainly 16th-century church combines Gothic, Baroque, and Renaissance elements. Inside, the curly, carved rood screen (1525–35), separating nave and chancel, is the only one of its kind in Paris. Note the uneven-floored chapel behind the choir, which can be reached via a cloister containing exquisite 17th-century stained glass. ✉ *Pl. de l'Abbé-Basset. Métro: Cardinal-Lemoine.*

**❻ St-Julien-le-Pauvre.** This tiny church was built at the same time as Notre-Dame (1165–1220), on a site where a succession of chapels once stood. The church belongs to a Greek Orthodox order today, but was originally named for St. Julian, bishop of Le Mans, who was nicknamed Le Pauvre after he gave all his money away. ✉ *rue St-Julien-le-Pauvre. Métro: St-Michel.*

**⓳ St-Louis-en-l'Ile.** The only church on the Ile St-Louis, built from 1664 to 1726 to the Baroque designs of architect Louis Le Vau, is lavishly furnished and has two unusual exterior features: its original pierced spire, holy in every sense, and an iron clock added in 1741. ✉ *rue St-Louis-en-l'Ile. Métro: Pont-Marie.*

**❼ St-Séverin.** This unusually wide, Flamboyant Gothic church dominates a Left Bank neighborhood filled with squares and pedestrian streets. Note the splendidly deviant spiraling column in the forest of pillars behind the altar. ⊠ *rue des Prêtres St-Séverin.* ⊙ *Weekdays 11–5:30, Sat. 11–10. Métro: St-Michel.*

**❾ Sorbonne.** Named after Robert de Sorbon, a medieval canon who founded a theological college here in 1253, this is one of the oldest universities in Europe. The church and university buildings were restored by Cardinal Richelieu in the 17th century, and the maze of amphitheaters, lecture rooms, and laboratories, along with the surrounding courtyards and narrow streets, retains a hallowed air. You can visit the main courtyard on rue de la Sorbonne and peek into the main lecture hall, a major meeting point during the tumultuous student upheavals of 1968. The square is dominated by the noble university church with cupola and Corinthian columns. Inside is the white-marble tomb of that ultimate crafty cleric, Cardinal Richelieu himself. ⊠ *rue de la Sorbonne. Métro: Cluny–La Sorbonne.*

## From Orsay to St-Germain

This section covers the Left Bank, from the Musée d'Orsay in the stately 7ᵉ arrondissement to the lively and colorful area around St-Germain-des-Prés in the 6ᵉ. The Musée d'Orsay, in a daringly converted Belle Epoque rail station on the Seine, houses one of the world's most spectacular arrays of Impressionist paintings. Farther along the river, the 18th-century Palais Bourbon, home to the National Assembly, sets the tone for the 7ᵉ arrondissement. Luxurious ministries and embassies—including the Hôtel Matignon, residence of the French prime minister—line the surrounding streets, their majestic scale in total keeping with the Hôtel des Invalides, whose gold-leafed dome climbs heavenward above the regal tomb of Napoléon. The splendid Rodin Museum is only a short walk away.

To the east, away from the splendor of the 7ᵉ, the boulevard St-Michel slices the Left Bank in two: on one side, the Latin Quarter (☞ The Islands and the Latin Quarter, *above*); on the other, the Faubourg St-Germain, named for St-Germain-des-Prés, the oldest church in Paris. The venerable church tower has long acted as a beacon for intellectuals, most famously during the 1950s when Albert Camus, Jean-

Paul Sartre, and Simone de Beauvoir ate and drank exis-
tentialism in the neighborhood cafés. Today most of the phi-
losophizing is done by tourists, yet a wealth of bookshops,
art stores, and antiques galleries ensure that St-Germain, as
the area is commonly known, retains its highbrow appeal.
In the southern part of this district is the city's most famous
and colorful park, the Jardin du Luxembourg.

*Numbers in the margin correspond to numbers on the
Orsay to St-Germain map; these numbers indicate a suggested path for sightseeing.*

## Sights to See

**❽ Atelier Delacroix** (Delacroix's Studio). The studio of artist
Eugène Delacroix (1798–1863) contains only a small collection of his sketches and drawings. But if you want to pay
homage to France's foremost Romantic painter, this museum is worth a visit. ⊠ *6 rue Furstenberg,* ☎ *01–43–54–
04–87.* 🔢 *15 frs, Sun. 10 frs.* 🕐 *Wed.–Mon. 9:30–5:30.
Métro: St-Germain-des-Prés.*

**❾ École Nationale des Beaux-Arts** (National Fine Arts College). In three large mansions near the Seine, this school—
today the breeding ground for painters, sculptors, and
architects—was once the site of a convent, founded in
1608. Only the church and cloister remained by the time
the Beaux-Arts school was established in 1816. Wander into
the courtyard and galleries of the school to see the casts and
copies of the statues stored here for safekeeping during the
Revolution. ⊠ *14 rue Bonaparte.* 🕐 *Daily 1–7. Métro: St-
Germain-des-Prés.*

NEED A        The popular **La Palette** café (⊠ 43 rue de Seine, ☎ 01–43–
BREAK?        26–68–15), on the corner of rue de Seine and rue Callot,
              has long been a favorite haunt of Beaux-Arts students.

**★ ❸ Hôtel des Invalides.** Les Invalides, as it is widely known, is
an outstanding monumental Baroque ensemble, designed by
Libéral Bruand in the 1670s at the behest of Louis XIV to
house wounded, or *invalid,* soldiers. Although no more
than a handful of old-timers live at the Invalides these days,
the army link remains in the form of the **Musée de l'Armée,**
a military museum. The **Musée des Plans-Reliefs,** also housed
here, contains a fascinating collection of old scale models

46

Atelier
Delacroix, 8
École
Nationale des
Beaux-Arts, 9
Hôtel des
Invalides, 3
Hôtel des
Monnaies, 11
Institut de
France, 10
Jardin du
Luxembourg, 13
Musée Maillol, 5
Musée
d'Orsay, 1
Musée Rodin, 4
Palais
Bourbon, 2
St-Germain-
des-Prés, 7
St-Sulpice, 6
Théâtre de
l'Odéon, 12

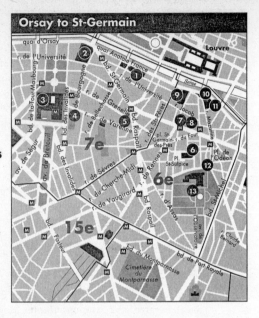

of French towns. The 17th-century **Église St-Louis des Invalides** is the Invalides' original church. More impressive is Jules Hardouin-Mansart's **Église du Dôme,** built onto the end of the church of St-Louis but blocked off from it in 1793. Napoléon's grandiose tomb is here. ⊠ *Pl. des Invalides,* ☎ *01–44–42–37–67.* 🎟 *37 frs.* ☉ *Apr.–Sept., daily 10–5:45; Oct.–Mar., daily 10–4:45. Métro: Latour-Maubourg.*

⑪ **Hôtel des Monnaies** (Mint). Louis XVI transferred the Royal Mint to this imposing mansion in the late 18th century. Although the mint was moved again, to Pessac, near Bordeaux, in 1973, weights and measures, medals, and limited-edition coins are still made here. The **Musée de la Monnaie** (Coin Museum) has an extensive collection of coins, documents, and engravings, plus a good shop. On Tuesday and Friday at 2 you can catch the coin metal craftsmen at work. ⊠ *11 quai de Conti,* ☎ *01–40–46–55–35.* 🎟 *20 frs.* ☉ *Tues.–Fri. 11–5:30, weekends noon–5:30. Métro: Pont-Neuf.*

⑩ **Institut de France** (French Institute). This is one of France's most revered cultural institutions, and its curved, dome-topped facade is one of the Left Bank's most impressive waterside sights. It was built as a college in 1661; at the beginning of the 19th century Napoléon had it transferred here from the Louvre. The Académie Française, the oldest of the five academies that compose the Institute, was created by Cardinal Richelieu in 1635. Its first major task (still unfinished) was to edit the definitive French dictionary; it is also charged with safeguarding the purity of the French language. ⊠ *Pl. de l'Institut.* ⊙ *Closed to the general public. Métro: Pont-Neuf.*

🕙 ⓭ **Jardin du Luxembourg** (Luxembourg Garden). One of the prettiest of Paris's few large parks, the Luxembourg Garden has fountains, ponds, trim hedges, precisely planted rows of trees, and gravel walks typical of the French fondness for formal landscaping. The 17th-century **Palais de Luxembourg** (Luxembourg Palace), overlooking the gardens, houses the French Senate and is not open to the public. It was built, like the gardens, for Maria de' Medici, widow of Henri IV. It was not completed until 1627, and Maria lived there for just five years before being expelled from France by Cardinal Richelieu in 1632. *Métro: Odéon; RER: Luxembourg.*

❺ **Musée Maillol.** Drawings, paintings, tapestries, and, above all, bronzes by Art Deco sculptor Aristide Maillol (1861–1944)—whose sleek, stylized nudes adorn the Tuileries—can be admired at this handsome town house, lovingly restored by his former muse Dina Vierny. ⊠ *61 rue de Grenelle,* ☎ *01-42-22-59-58.* ⊡ *40 frs.* ⊙ *Wed.–Mon. 11–6. Métro: Rue du Bac.*

❶ **Musée d'Orsay.** In a stylishly converted train station, the Orsay Museum—devoted to the arts (mainly French) spanning the period 1848–1914—is one of the city's most popular. The main artistic attraction is the Impressionists: Renoir, Sisley, Pissarro, and Monet are all well represented. The post-Impressionists—Cézanne, van Gogh, Gauguin, and Toulouse-Lautrec—are on the top floor. On the ground floor you'll find the work of Manet, the powerful realism of Courbet, and the delicate nuances of Degas. If you prefer more academic paintings, look for Puvis de Chavannes's larger-than-life classical canvases. And if you're excited by more modern developments, look for the early 20th-century Fauves (meaning "wild beasts," the name given them by an outraged critic in 1905)—particularly Matisse, Derain, and Vlaminck. Thought-provoking sculptures also lurk at every turn. ⊠ *1 rue de Bellechasse*, ☎ *01–40–49–48–14.* ▧ *40 frs, Sun. 30 frs.* ☉ *Tues.–Wed. and Fri.–Sat. 10–6, Thurs. 10–9:45, Sun. 9–6. Métro: Solférino; RER: Musée d'Orsay.*

NEED A
BREAK?

Find respite from the overwhelming collection of art in the **Musée d'Orsay Café** behind one of the giant station clocks, close to the Impressionist galleries on the top floor.

❹ **Musée Rodin.** The 18th-century Hôtel Biron makes a gracious setting for the sculpture of Auguste Rodin (1840–1917). You'll doubtless recognize the seated *Le Penseur* (*The Thinker*), with his elbow resting on his knee, and the passionate *Le Baiser* (*The Kiss*). From the upper rooms, which contain some fine if murky paintings by Rodin's friend Eugène Carrière (1849–1906) and some fine sculptures by Rodin's mistress, Camille Claudel (1864–1943), you can see the large garden behind the house. Don't skip the garden: It is exceptional both for its rosebushes (more than 2,000 of them) and for its sculpture. ⊠ *77 rue de Varenne*, ☎ *01–44–18–61–10.* ▧ *28 frs, Sun. 18 frs; gardens only 5 frs.* ☉ *Easter–Oct., Tues.–Sun. 10–5:45; Nov.–Easter, Tues.–Sun. 10–4:45. Métro: Varenne.*

❷ **Palais Bourbon.** The most prominent feature of the home of the Assemblée Nationale (French Parliament) is its colonnaded facade, commissioned by Napoléon. ⊠ *Pl. du Palais-Bourbon.* ☉ *During temporary exhibits only. Métro: Assemblée Nationale.*

❼ **St-Germain-des-Prés.** Paris's oldest church was first built to shelter a relic of the true cross, brought back from Spain in AD 542. The chancel was enlarged and the church then consecrated by Pope Alexander III in 1163; the tall, sturdy tower—a Left Bank landmark—dates from this period. The church stages superb organ concerts and recitals. ⊠ *Pl. St-Germain.* ☉ *Weekdays 8–7:30, weekends 8–9. Métro: St-Germain-des-Prés.*

❻ **St-Sulpice.** Dubbed the "Cathedral of the Left Bank," this enormous 17th-century church is of note for the powerful

Delacroix frescoes in the first chapel on the right. The 18th-century facade was never finished, and its unequal towers add a playful touch to an otherwise sober design. ⊠ *Pl. St-Sulpice. Métro: St-Sulpice.*

**⑫ Théâtre de l'Odéon.** At the north end of the Luxembourg Gardens, on Place de l'Odéon, sits the colonnaded Odéon Theater. It was established in 1792 to house the Comédie Française troupe; the original building was destroyed by fire in 1807. Since World War II it has specialized in 20th-century productions and was the base for Jean-Louis Barrault's and Madeleine Renaud's theater company, the Théâtre de France, until they fell out of favor with the authorities for their alleged role in spurring on student revolutionaries in May 1968. Today, the theater is the French home of the Theater of Europe and stages excellent productions by major foreign companies, sometimes in English (☞ Chapter 5). ⊠ *Pl. de l'Odéon,* ☎ *01–44–41–36–36. Métro: Odéon.*

## Montparnasse

One and one-half kilometers (1 mile) south of the Seine is the district of Montparnasse, named after Mount Parnassus, the Greek mountain associated with the worship of Apollo and the Muses. Montparnasse's cultural heyday came in the first four decades of the 20th century, when it replaced Montmartre as *the* place for painters and poets to live, which prompted the launch of a string of artsy brasseries along the district's main thoroughfare, the broad boulevard du Montparnasse. The boulevard may lack poetic charm these days, but nightlife stays the pace, as bars, clubs, restaurants, and cinemas crackle with energy beneath Europe's second-tallest high-rise: the 59-story Tour Montparnasse. Although the tower itself is a typically bland product of the early 1970s, of note only for the view from the top, several more-adventurous buildings have risen in its wake: Ricardo Boffil's semicircular Amphithéâtre housing complex, the glass-cubed Cartier Center for Contemporary Art, and the Montparnasse train station with its giant glass facade and designer garden above the tracks. If you have a deeper feel for history, you may prefer the Baroque church of Val-de-Grâce or the quiet Montparnasse Cemetery.

*Numbers in the margin correspond to numbers on the Montparnasse map; these numbers indicate a suggested path for sightseeing.*

## Sights to See

**⑥ Catacombs.** Enter the Paris catacombs, originally built by the Romans to quarry stone, from Place Denfert-Rochereau. The square was named after General Denfert-Rochereau (d. 1878) in 1879, the heroic Governor of Belfort during the Prussian invasion of 1870. The square had been known as Place d'Enfer (Hell Square) until it was punningly renamed after the general. The catacombs, which tunnel under much of the Left Bank, were used to store millions of skeletons from disused graveyards; during World War II, they were the headquarters of the French Resistance. Bring a flashlight. ✉ *1 Pl. Denfert-Rochereau,* ☎ *01–43–22–47–63.* 🎟 *27 frs.* ☻ *Tues.–Fri. 2–4, weekends 9–11 and 2–4. Guided tours on Wed. at 2:45; 20 frs extra. Métro and RER: Denfert-Rochereau.*

**⑤ Cimetière du Montparnasse** (Montparnasse Cemetery). This cemetery is not picturesque, but it contains many of the quarter's most illustrious residents: Charles Baudelaire, Auguste Bartholdi, Jean-Paul Sartre, Man Ray, Samuel Beckett, Jean Seberg, and Serge Gainsbourg. ✉ *Entrances at rue Froidevaux, bd. Edgar-Quinet. Métro: Raspail, Gaîté.*

**⑧ Closerie des Lilas.** Now a pricey bar-restaurant, the Closerie remains a staple of all literary tours of Paris. Commemorative plaques fastened to the bar mark the places where literati like Baudelaire, Verlaine, Hemingway, and Apollinaire used to station themselves. Although the lilacs (*lilas*) have gone from the terrace, it still opens onto a garden wall of luxuriant evergreen foliage, and is as crowded in the summer as it ever was in the '30s. ✉ *171 bd. du Montparnasse,* ☎ *01–43–26–70–50. Métro: Vavin; RER: Port-Royal.*

**⑦ Fondation Cartier** (Cartier Foundation). Architect Jean Nouvel's eye-catching giant glass cubicle is a suitable setting for the temporary, thought-provoking shows of contemporary art organized here by jewelry giant Cartier. ✉ *261 bd. Raspail,* ☎ *01–42–18–56–50.* 🎟 *30 frs.* ☻ *Tues.–Sun. noon–8. Métro: Raspail.*

**51**

Catacombs, **6**
Cimetière du
Montparnasse, **5**
Closerie des
Lilas, **8**
Fondation
Cartier, **7**
Jardin
Atlantique, **3**
Place de
Catalogne, **4**
Place du 18-
Juin-1940, **1**
Tour
Montparnasse, **2**
Val de Grâce, **9**

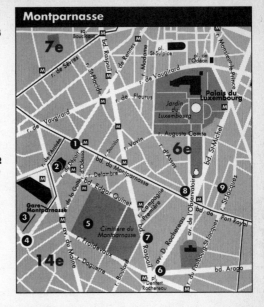

**3** **Jardin Atlantique** (Atlantic Garden). This small park, which
opened in 1994, was planted on a concourse constructed
over the first 100 yards of the tracks leading to the Gare
Montparnasse. It features an assortment of trees and plants
from countries on the Atlantic Ocean. What looks like a
quirky metal sculpture in the middle of the park is, in fact,
a weather observatory with a battery of flickering lights chart-
ing temperature, wind speed, and rainfall. ⊠ *Pont des Cinq-
Martyrs-du-Lycée-Buffon. Métro: Montparnasse-Bienvenüe.*

**4** **Place de Catalogne.** This square is dominated by Ricardo
Boffil's monumental **Amphithéâtre** housing complex, with
its chunky reinvention of classical detail. Just behind is the
turn-of-the-century church of **Notre-Dame du Travail**,
whose riveted iron-and-steel framework was meant to symbolize the work ethos enshrouded in the church's name.
*Métro: Gaîté.*

**1** **Place du 18-Juin-1940.** This square, beneath Tour Montparnasse (☞ below) is named for the date of the radio speech
Charles de Gaulle broadcast from London, urging the

French to resist the Germans after the Nazi invasion of May 1940. It was here that German military governor Dietrich von Choltitz surrendered to the Allies in August 1944, ignoring Hitler's orders to destroy the city as he withdrew. A plaque on the wall commemorates the event. *Métro: Montparnasse-Bienvenüse.*

**②** **Tour Montparnasse** (Montparnasse Tower). As Europe's second-tallest skyscraper, completed in 1973, this 685-ft tower offers a stupendous view of Paris from its open-air roof terrace. Fifty-two of the 59 stories are taken up by offices and a vast commercial complex, including a Galeries Lafayette department store, spreads over the first floor. Banal by day, the tower becomes Montparnasse's neon-lighted beacon at night. ⊠ *33 av. du Maine.* ⊠ *46 frs.* ☉ *Apr.–Sept., daily 9:30 AM–11:30 PM; Oct.–Mar., Sun.–Thurs. 9:30 AM–10:30 PM, Fri.–Sat. 9:30 AM–11 PM. Métro: Montparnasse-Bienvenüse.*

**⑨** **Val de Grâce.** This imposing 17th-century Left Bank church was commissioned by Anne of Austria and designed by François Mansart. Its powerfully rhythmic two-story facade rivals the Dôme Church at the Invalides as the city's most striking example of Italianate Baroque. ⊠ *1 Pl. Alphonse-Laveran. RER: Port-Royal.*

## Montmartre

On a dramatic rise above the city is Montmartre, site of the Sacré-Coeur Basilica and home to a once-thriving artistic community. Although the fabled nightlife of old Montmartre has fizzled down to some glitzy nightclubs and porn shows, Montmartre still exudes history and Gallic charm. Windmills once dotted Montmartre (often referred to by Parisians as *La Butte,* meaning "mound"). They were set up here not just because the hill was a good place to catch the wind—at more than 300 ft, it's the highest point in the city—but because Montmartre was covered with wheat fields and quarries right up to the end of the 19th century. Today only two of the original 20 windmills remain. Visiting Montmartre means negotiating a lot of steep streets and flights of steps. The crown atop this urban peak, the Sacré-Coeur Basilica, is something of an architectural oddity. It has been called everything from grotesque to sublime; its silhouette, viewed from afar at dusk or sunrise, looks more like a mosque than a cathedral.

*Numbers in the margin correspond to numbers on the Montmartre map; these numbers indicate a suggested path for sightseeing.*

## Sights to See

**⑧ Bateau-Lavoir** (Boat Wash House). Montmartre poet Max Jacob coined the name for the original building on this site (which burned down in 1970), saying it resembled a boat and that the warren of artists' studios within was perpetually paint-splattered and in need of a good hosing down. It was here that Pablo Picasso and Georges Braque made their first bold stabs at the concept of Cubism. The new building also contains art studios, but is the epitome of poured-concrete drabness. ⊠ *13 Pl. Émile-Goudeau. Métro: Abbesses.*

**⑩ Espace Dalí** (Dalí Center). Some of Salvador Dalí's less familiar works are among the 25 sculptures and 300 prints housed in this museum with an atmosphere that is meant to approximate the surreal experience. ⊠ *11 rue Poulbot,* ☎ *01–42–64–40–10.* ☞ *35 frs.* ☉ *Spring–fall, daily 10–6; summer, daily 10–8. Métro: Abbesses.*

**⑭ Lapin Agile.** This bar-cabaret, originally one of the raunchiest haunts in Montmartre, got its curious name—the Nimble Rabbit—when the owner, André Gill, hung up a sign of a laughing rabbit jumping out of a saucepan clutching a bottle of wine. Locals christened it the Lapin à Gill, meaning "Gill's rabbit." When, in 1886, it was sold to cabaret singer Jules Jouy, he called it the Lapin Agile, which has the same pronunciation in French as Lapin à Gill. In 1903 the premises were bought by the most celebrated cabaret entrepreneur of them all, Aristide Bruand, depicted by Toulouse-Lautrec in a series of famous posters. ⊠ *22 rue des Saules,* ☎ *01–46–06–85–87. Métro: Lamarck-Caulaincourt.*

**⑤ Moulin de la Galette** (Biscuit Windmill). This is one of two remaining windmills in Montmartre. It was once the focal point of an open-air cabaret (made famous in a painting by Renoir). Rumor has it that in 1814 the miller Debray,

**54**

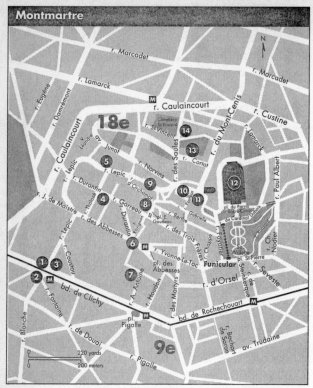

# Montmartre

Bateau-Lavoir, **8**

Espace Dalí, **10**

Lapin Agile, **14**

Moulin de la Galette, **5**

Moulin Rouge, **1**

Musée de l'Erotisme, **3**

Musée de Montmartre, **13**

Place des Abbesses, **6**

Place Blanche, **2**

Place Jean-Baptiste-Clément, **9**

Place du Tertre, **11**

Sacré-Coeur, **12**

Studio 28, **4**

Théâtre Libre, **7**

who had struggled in vain to defend the windmill from invading Cossacks, was then strung up on its sails and spun to death by the invaders. Unfortunately, it is privately owned and can only be admired from the street below. ⊠ *rue Tholozé. Métro: Abbesses.*

**①** **Moulin Rouge** (Red Windmill). This world-famous cabaret was built in 1885 as a windmill, then transformed into a dance hall in 1900. Those wild, early days were immortalized by Toulouse-Lautrec in his posters and paintings. It still trades shamelessly on the notion of Paris as a city of sin: If you fancy a Vegas-style night out, this is the place to go. ⊠ *82 bd. de Clichy,* ☎ *01–53–09–82–82. Métro: Blanche.*

**③** **Musée de l'Erotisme** (Erotic Art Museum). Opened in 1997, this museum claims to offer "a prestigious showcase for every kind of erotic fantasy." Its 2,000 works of art—some might question that term—range from Peruvian potteries, African carvings, and Indian miniatures to Nepalese bronzes, Chinese ivories, and Japanese prints. ⊠ *72 bd. de Clichy,* ☎ *01–42–58–28–73.* ▥ *40 frs.* ☉ *Daily 10 AM–2 AM. Métro: Blanche.*

**⑬** **Musée de Montmartre** (Montmartre Museum). In its turn-of-the-century heyday, Montmartre's historical museum was home to an illustrious group of painters, writers, and assorted cabaret artists. Foremost among them were Renoir and Maurice Utrillo. The museum also provides a view of the tiny **vineyard**—the only one in Paris—on neighboring rue des Saules. A token 125 gallons of wine are still produced every year. ⊠ *12 rue Cortot,* ☎ *01–46–06–61–11.* ▥ *25 frs.* ☉ *Tues.–Sun. 11–6. Métro: Lamarck-Caulaincourt.*

**⑥** **Place des Abbesses.** This triangular square is typical of the picturesque, slightly countrified style that has made Montmartre famous. The entrance to the Abbesses métro station, a curving, sensuous mass of delicate iron, is one of two original Art Nouveau entrance canopies left in Paris. *Métro: Abbesses.*

**②** **Place Blanche.** The name Place Blanche—White Square—comes from the clouds of chalky dust that used to be churned up by the carts that carried wheat and crushed flour from the nearby windmills, including the Moulin Rouge. *Métro: Blanche.*

**⑨ Place Jean-Baptiste-Clément.** Painter Amedeo Modigliani (1884–1920) had a studio here at No. 7. Some say he was the greatest Italian artist of the 20th century, fusing the genius of the Renaissance with the modernity of Cézanne and Picasso. He claimed that he would drink himself to death—he eventually did—and chose the right part of town to do it in. Look for the octagonal tower at the north end of the square; it's all that's left of Montmartre's first water tower, built around 1840 to boost the area's feeble water supply. ⊠ *Pl. Jean-Baptiste-Clément. Métro: Abbesses.*

**⑪ Place du Tertre.** This tumbling square (*tertre* means "hillock") regains its village atmosphere only in the winter, when the branches of the plane trees sketch traceries against the sky. At any other time of year you'll be confronted by crowds of tourists and a swarm of third-rate artists clamoring to do your portrait (if one of them produces an unsolicited portrait, you are not obligated to buy it). **La Mère Catherine,** on one corner of the square, was a favorite with the Russian Cossacks who occupied Paris in 1814. They couldn't have suspected that, by banging on the table and yelling "bistro" (Russian for quickly), they were inventing a new breed of French restaurant. *Métro: Abbesses.*

NEED A     **Patachou** (⊠ 9 Pl. du Tertre, ☎ 01–42–51–06–06), serving
BREAK?     exquisite if expensive cakes and teas, sounds the one classy
           note on Place du Tertre.

**⑫ Sacré-Coeur.** The Sacred Heart Basilica was erected as a sort of national guilt offering in expiation for the blood shed during the Paris Commune and Franco-Prussian War in 1870–71 and was largely financed by French Catholics fearful of an anticlerical backlash under the new republican regime. The basilica was not consecrated until 1919. Stylistically, the Sacré-Coeur borrows elements from Romanesque and Byzantine models. The gloomy, cavernous interior is worth visiting for its golden mosaics; climb to the top of the dome for the view of Paris. ⊠ *Pl. du Parvis-du-Sacré-Coeur. Métro: Anvers.*

**④ Studio 28.** What looks like no more than a generic little movie theater has a distinguished dramatic history: When it opened in 1928, it was the first purposely built for *art et essai,* or experimental theater, in the world. Over the years, the movies of directors like Jean Cocteau, François Truffaut, and Orson Welles have been shown here before their official premieres. ✉ *10 rue Tholozé,* ☎ *01–46–06–36–07. Métro: Abbesses.*

**7 Théâtre Libre** (Free Theater). Founded in 1887 by director André Antoine (1858–1943), this theater was immensely influential in popularizing the work of iconoclastic young playwrights such as Ibsen and Strindberg. Antoine later became the director of the Odéon Theater in 1906. ✉ *37 rue André-Antoine. Métro: Abbesses.*

# 3 Dining

Revised
and
updated by
Alexander
Lobrano

**P**ARIS REMAINS THE ULTIMATE gourmet destination. This listing includes restaurants of a variety of styles and price levels, from formal dining rooms serving haute cuisine to fashionable bistros serving classical and contemporary cooking. Generally, Paris restaurants are open from noon to about 2 and from 7:30 or 8 to 10 or 10:30. It's best to make reservations, particularly in summer, although the reviews only state when reservations are absolutely essential. If you want no-smoking seating, make this clear; the mandatory no-smoking area is sometimes limited to a very few tables. Brasseries have longer hours and often serve all day and late into the evening; some are open 24 hours. Assume a restaurant is open every day unless otherwise indicated. Surprisingly, many prestigious restaurants close on Saturday as well as Sunday. July and August are the most common months for annual closings, although Paris in August is no longer the wasteland it once was.

Most restaurants have two basic types of menu: *à la carte* and *prix fixe* (fixed price, or *un menu*), which is usually the best value, though choices are limited. Except for brasseries, wine bars, and other simple places, it's inappropriate to order just one dish, as you'll understand when you see the waiter's expression. The popular *menu dégustation* (tasting menu), with many small courses, allows for a wide sampling of the chef's offerings. In general, consider the season and the daily specials when ordering.

Although prices include tax and tip by law, pocket change left on the table in simple places, or an additional 5% in better restaurants, is appreciated. Places where a jacket and tie are de rigueur are noted. Otherwise, use common sense—jeans and T-shirts are not suitable in Paris restaurants, nor are shorts or running clothes, except in the most casual bistros and cafés.

| CATEGORY | COST* |
|----------|-------|
| $$$$ | over 550 frs |
| $$$ | 300 frs–550 frs |
| $$ | 175 frs–300 frs |
| $ | under 175 frs |

*per person for a three-course meal, including 20.6% tax and service but not drinks*

## Restaurants

### 1ᵉʳ Arrondissement (Louvre/Les Halles)

FRENCH

$$$$  ✕ **Le Grand Véfour.** Luminaries from Napoléon to Colette to Jean Cocteau frequented this intimate address under the arcades of the Palais-Royal; you can request to be seated at their preferred tables. A sumptuously decorated restaurant, with mirrored ceiling and painted glass panels, it is perhaps the prettiest in Paris, and its 18th-century origins make it one of the oldest. Chef Guy Martin impresses with his unique blend of sophisticated yet rustic dishes, including foie gras–stuffed ravioli and truffled veal sweetbreads. ⊠ *17 rue Beaujolais,* ☎ *01–42–96–56–27. Reservations essential 1 wk in advance. Jacket and tie. AE, DC, MC, V. Closed weekends and Aug. Métro: Palais-Royal.*

$$  ✕ **Restaurant du Palais-Royal.** Tucked away in the northern corner of the magnificent Palais-Royal garden, this pleasant bistro has good food and a lovely terrace. A salad of baby scallops and pleurotus mushrooms in a balsamic vinaigrette is among the interesting contemporary dishes. ⊠ *Jardin du Palais-Royal, 110 Galerie Valois,* ☎ *01–40–20–00–27. AE, MC, V. Closed Sun. No lunch Sat. Métro: Palais-Royal.*

$–$$  ✕ **Aux Crus de Bourgogne.** This delightfully old-fashioned bistro, with its bright lights and red-check tablecloths, attracts a lively crowd. It opened in 1932 and quickly became popular by serving two luxury items—foie gras and cold lobster with homemade mayonnaise—at surprisingly low prices, a tradition that happily continues. ⊠ *3 rue Bachaumont,* ☎ *01–42–33–48–24. V. Closed weekends and Aug. Métro: Sentier.*

## 2ᵉ Arrondissement (La Bourse)

FRENCH

**$$** ✕ **Chez Georges.** The traditional bistro cooking is good—herring, sole, kidneys, steak, and *frîtes* (fries)—but the atmosphere is better. A wood-paneled entry leads you to an elegant and unpretentious dining room where one long, white-clothed stretch of table lines the mirrored walls. ⊠ *1 rue du Mail,* ☎ *01–42–60–07–11. AE, DC, MC, V. Closed Sun. and Aug. Métro: Sentier.*

**$$** ✕ **Le Vaudeville.** One of Jean-Paul Bucher's seven Parisian brasseries, Le Vaudeville is filled with well-dressed Parisians (many from the Stock Exchange across the street) and is a good value, thanks to its assortment of prix-fixe menus. Shellfish, house-smoked salmon, and desserts such as profiteroles are particularly fine. Enjoy the handsome 1930s decor and joyful dining until 2 AM daily. ⊠ *29 rue Vivienne,* ☎ *01–40–20–04–62. AE, DC, MC, V. Closed Dec. 24. Métro: Bourse.*

## 3ᵉ Arrondissement (Beaubourg/Marais)

FRENCH

**$** ✕ **Au Bascou.** Gregarious proprietor Jean-Guy Lousteau enthusiastically shares his knowledge of the wines of southwest France at this fashionable little bistro. The sturdy, savory cuisine of the Basque Country stars on the menu; the country ham and cod with broccoli puree are particularly flavorful. ⊠ *38 rue Réaumur,* ☎ *01–42–72–69–25. MC, V. Closed weekends. Métro: Arts et Métiers.*

**$** ✕ **Chez Jenny.** Since the installation of a rotisserie grill, this restaurant has become *the* place for some of the best choucroute in the capital. The sauerkraut, delivered weekly by a private supplier in Alsace, is garnished with a variety of charcuterie and a big grilled ham knuckle. For dessert, the perfectly aged Muenster cheese and homemade blueberry tart are good choices. The ambience is lively. ⊠ *39 bd. du Temple,* ☎ *01–42–74–75–75. AE, DC, MC, V. Métro: République.*

NORTH AFRICAN

**$** ✕ **Chez Omar.** Come here for couscous, the signature North African dish, with grilled lamb, *merguez* (spicy, red) sausage, or chicken; portions are generous. The restaurant, in a former turn-of-the-century bistro, is popular with a fashion-

62

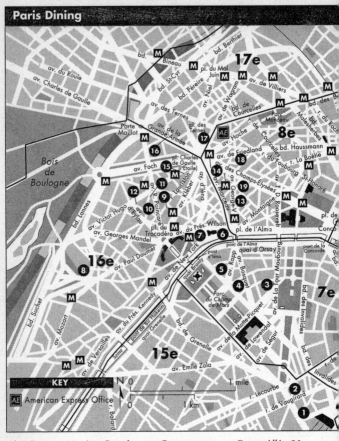

## Paris Dining

KEY

**AE** American Express Office

N

0                              1 mile

0                              1 km

Alain Ducasse, **11**

Alcazar, **43**

L'Ambroisie, **39**

Anacréon, **56**

Androuët, **20**

Astier, **33**

Au Bascou, **31**

Au Bon
Accueil, **5**

Au Camelot, **36**

Au Trou
Gascon, **51**

Aux Crus de
Bourgogne, **30**

Baracane, **41**

La Bastide
Odéon, **48**

Bistrot
d'Hubert, **1**

Bofinger, **42**

Brasserie Flo, **24**

La Butte
Chaillot, **9**

Campagne et
Provence, **49**

Chardenoux, **40**

Chartier, **25**

Les Chauffeurs, **8**

Chez Georges, **27**

Chez Jenny, **32**

Chez Maître
Paul, **47**

Chez Michel, **22**

Chez Omar, **34**

Chez René, **50**

Contre-Allée, **54**

La Coupole, **53**

Les Élysées, **14**

L'Espadon
Bleu, **44**

La Fermette
Marbeuf, **13**

Le Grand
Véfour, **29**

Le Grizzli, **37**

Guy Savoy, **17**

Jamin, **7**

Le Moulin
à Vins, **21**

Paul Minchelli, **3**

Le Petit Rétro, **12**

Philippe
Detourbe, **2**

Pierre
Gagnaire, **6**

Prunier, **15**

Le Relais
du Parc, **10**

Le Reminet, **46**

Le Repaire de
Cartouche, **35**

Le Restaurant
d'Eric Frechon, **23**

Restaurant du
Palais-Royal, **28**

Sébillon, **19**

Le Square
Trousseau, **52**

Taillevent, **18**

Le Terroir, **55**

Le Timgad, **16**

Le Vaudeville, **26**

Il Vicolo, **38**

Le Vieux Bistro, **45**

Le Violon
d'Ingres, **4**

able crowd. Proprietor Omar Guerida is famously friendly and speaks English. ⊠ *47 rue de Bretagne,* ☏ *01–42–72–36–26. MC, V. No lunch Sun. Métro: Filles du Calvaire.*

## 4ᵉ Arrondissement (Marais/Ile St-Louis)

FRENCH

**$$$$**  ✕ **L'Ambroisie.** At this tiny, romantic restaurant on Place des Vosges, chef-owner Bernard Pacaud serves refined, oft-imitated cuisine, such as red bell pepper mousse, and braised oxtail. The jewellike Italianate setting of flowers, tapestries, and subdued lighting adds to the pleasure of eating here. ⊠ *9 pl. des Vosges,* ☏ *01–42–78–51–45. Reservations essential 1 month in advance. MC, V. Closed Sun., Mon., Aug., and mid-Feb. Métro: St-Paul.*

**$$**  ✕ **Le Grizzli.** It's said that this turn-of-the-century bistro used to have dancing bears out front—thus the name. The owner gets many of his ingredients—especially the wonderful ham and cheeses—from his native Auvergne. Several dishes are cooked on a hot slate, including the salmon and the lamb. There's an interesting selection of wines from southwest France. ⊠ *7 rue St-Martin,* ☏ *01–48–87–77–56. MC, V. Closed Sun. Métro: Châtelet.*

**$$**  ✕ **Le Vieux Bistro.** Overlook the touristy location next to Notre-Dame and the corny name, the Old Bistro. This place really *is* generations old, and its menu is full of bistro classics, such as beef fillet with marrow, and tart Tatin. The decor is nondescript, but the frequently fancy crowd doesn't seem to notice. ⊠ *14 rue du Cloître-Notre-Dame,* ☏ *01–43–54–18–95. MC, V. Métro: Hôtel de Ville.*

**$–$$**  ✕ **Bofinger.** One of the oldest, most beautiful, and most popular brasseries in Paris has generally improved since brasserie maestro Jean-Paul Bucher took over. Settle in to one of the tables dressed in crisp white linens, under the gorgeous Art Nouveau glass cupola, and enjoy fine classic brasserie fare, such as oysters, grilled sole, or fillet of lamb. The house Muscadet is a good white wine, the Fleurie is a pleasant red. Note that the no-smoking section here is not only enforced, but is also in the prettiest part of the restaurant. ⊠ *5–7 rue de la Bastille,* ☏ *01–42–72–87–82. AE, DC, MC, V. Métro: Bastille.*

**$**  ✕ **Baracane.** The owner of this small, simple spot oversees the menu of robust specialties of his native southwest

France, including rabbit confit, veal tongue, and pear poached in wine and cassis. The prix-fixe menus are a good value. ✉ *38 rue des Tournelles,* ☎ *01–42–71–43–33. MC, V. Closed Sun. No lunch Sat. Métro: Bastille.*

### ITALIAN

**$$** ✗ **Il Vicolo.** Low-key but stylish, with a trendy, young crowd, this restaurant serves authentic and very good contemporary Italian cuisine—it's ideal for a night off from French food. The spicy chickpea soup is delicious, as is the Livorno-style red mullet, served in a sauce of wine and herbs. Delicious desserts and a nice Italian wine list finish off the evening. ✉ *8 rue de Jouy,* ☎ *01–42–78–38–86. MC, V. Closed Sun., Mon. Métro: St-Paul.*

## 5e Arrondissement (Latin Quarter)

### FRENCH

**$$** ✗ **Campagne et Provence.** On the quai across from Notre-Dame, this very pleasant little restaurant has a rustic Provençal look and a menu to match, which includes grilled John Dory with preserved fennel and peppers stuffed with cod and eggplant. ✉ *25 quai de la Tournelle,* ☎ *01–43–54–05–17. MC, V. Closed Sun. No lunch Sat., Mon. Métro: Maubert-Mutualité.*

**$$** ✗ **Chez René.** This reliable address at the eastern end of boulevard St-Germain has satisfied three generations of Parisians, who count on finding dishes from Burgundy, such as *boeuf Bourguignon* (beef stewed in wine) and coq au vin. The dining rooms are cozy, with red-leatherette banquettes and white honeycomb-tile floors. ✉ *14 bd. St-Germain,* ☎ *01–43–54–30–23. MC, V. Closed Sun., Aug., and late Dec.–early Jan. No lunch Sat. Métro: Cardinal Lemoine.*

**$** ✗ **Le Reminet.** The atmosphere is relaxed at this unusually
★ good bistro in a small, narrow room with stone walls, though chandeliers and mirrors add an unexpected note of elegance. The menu changes regularly and displays the young chef's talent with dishes like a salad of scallops, greens, and sesame seeds, and roasted guinea hen with buttered Savoy cabbage. If available, try the luscious caramelized pears with cream. The lower-priced wines have been carefully chosen and are a good value. ✉ *3 rue des Grands-Degrés,* ☎ *01–44–07–04–24. AE, MC, V. Closed Mon. and Tues. Métro: Maubert-Mutualité.*

## 6° Arrondissement (St-Germain)

FRENCH

**$$** ✕ **Alcazar.** Englishman Sir Terence Conran's stunning, large new brasserie is one of the chicest and liveliest spots in town. Young French chef Guillaume Lutard has created a regularly changing, appealingly classic menu. Note that there's a separate and less expensive bar menu—a good option for a quick, casual bite. ⊠ *62 rue Mazarine,* ☎ *01–53–10–19–99. Reservations essential. AE, DC, MC, V. Métro: Odéon.*

**$$** ✕ **La Bastide Odéon.** This little corner of Provence in Paris
★ is just a few steps from the Luxembourg Gardens. A sunny yellow restaurant with old oak tables and chairs, it's one of the best places to sample Mediterranean cuisine. Chef Gilles Ajuelos cooks fine fish dishes; wonderful pastas, such as tagliatelle in *pistou* (basil and pine nuts) with wild mushrooms; and delightful main courses, like roast suckling pig, and cod with capers. The best bet on the slightly pricey wine list is the red Côteaux du Tricastin. ⊠ *7 rue Corneille,* ☎ *01–43–26–03–65. MC, V. Closed Sun., Mon. Métro: Odéon; RER: Luxembourg.*

**$** ✕ **Chez Maître Paul.** A few steps from the Odéon, this is a great place to discover the little-known cooking of the Jura and Franche-Comté. Though sturdy, this cuisine appeals to modern palates, too. ⊠ *12 rue Monsieur-le-Prince,* ☎ *01–43–54–74–59. AE, DC, MC, V. Metro: Odéon.*

SEAFOOD

**$$** ✕ **L'Espadon Bleu.** Chef Jacques Cagna's moderately priced seafood restaurant is a good spot to drop anchor in St-Germain. Yellow walls, blue beams, and mosaic tables with the restaurant's namesake, a blue swordfish, create a stylish nautical feel. The prix-fixe menu is a great deal. ⊠ *25 rue des Grands Augustins,* ☎ *01–46–33–00–85. Reservations essential. AE, MC, V. Closed Sun. and Mon. No lunch Sat. Métro: Odéon.*

## 7° Arrondissement (Invalides/École Militaire)

FRENCH

**$$–$$$** ✕ **Le Violon d'Ingres.** A diverse crowd comes to sample the
★ regularly revised menu of chef Christian Constant, formerly of the Hôtel Crillon (☞ Chapter 4). Sample dishes include cream of pumpkin soup with sheep's cheese and

guinea hen on a bed of diced turnips. It's the perfect place for a dinner out on the town. ⊠ *135 rue St-Dominique,* ☎ *01–45–44–15–05. Reservations essential. AE, DC, MC, V. Closed Sun.–Mon. Métro: École-Militaire.*

**$–$$** ✕ **Au Bon Accueil.** If you want to see what well-heeled Parisians like to eat these days, book a table at this popular bistro as soon as you get to town. The excellent, reasonably priced *cuisine du marché* (daily menu based on what's in the markets) has made it a hit. ⊠ *14 rue de Montessuy,* ☎ *01–47–05–46–11. Reservations essential. MC, V. Closed Sun. Métro, RER: Pont de l'Alma.*

SEAFOOD

**$$$–$$$$** ✕ **Paul Minchelli.** Minchelli is a minimalist who believes that seasonings should not distract from the taste of his impeccably fresh—and very expensive—catch of the day. The baby clams with garlic and fiery espelette peppers as well as the sea bass drizzled with lemon and olive oil are just two of his wonderful dishes. The dressy dining room with gentle lighting and witty trompe l'oeil "views" out of "portholes" is the backdrop for a very stylish crowd, often sprinkled with celebrities. ⊠ *54 bd. de La Tour-Maubourg,* ☎ *01–47–05– 89–86. MC, V. Closed Sun., Mon. Métro: École Militaire.*

# 8ᵉ Arrondissement (Champs-Élysées)

FRENCH

**$$$$** ✕ **Les Élysées.** Chef Alain Solivères is a passionate cook
★ whose reputation continues to grow. Not only is his food—which changes seasonally and draws inspiration from southern France, the Basque Country, Bordeaux, and Languedoc—exquisite, but service is also impeccable, and the intimate dining room beautiful. ⊠ *In Hôtel Vernet, 25 rue Vernet,* ☎ *01–47–23–43–10. AE, DC, MC, V. Reservations essential. Closed weekends. Métro: George-V.*

**$$$$** ✕ **Pierre Gagnaire.** In a single dish, legendary chef Pierre
★ Gagnaire sensationally brings together unexpected tastes and textures. Two intriguing dishes from a recent menu—it changes seasonally—included duck foie gras wrapped in bacon, and sea bass in herbs with tiny clams. The only negatives are the amateurish service and the brief wine list. ⊠ *6 rue de Balzac,* ☎ *01–44–35–18–25. Reservations essential. AE, DC, MC, V. Closed Sun. Métro: Charles-de-Gaulle–Étoile.*

$$$$ ✕ **Taillevent.** Many say this is the best restaurant in Paris—and dining in the paneled rooms of this mid-19th-century mansion is certainly a sublime experience. Service is exceptional, the wine list remarkable, and the classical French cuisine usually perfect. ⊠ *15 rue Lamennais,* ☎ *01–45–63–39–94. Reservations 3–4 wks in advance essential. Jacket and tie. AE, MC, V. Closed weekends and Aug. Métro: Charles-de-Gaulle–Étoile.*

$$ ✕ **Androuët.** The ideal address if you're mad for cheese, this restaurant has been proudly serving a vast assortment of beautifully aged *fromages* (cheeses) from all over France for almost a century. If you really want a cheese-filled feast, or just want to learn more about the stuff, order the tasting menu, which takes you through the seven main French types. Also available are a variety of good dishes like lobster with Roquefort and Camembert croquettes. ⊠ *41 rue Arsène-Houssaye,* ☎ *01–42–89–95–00. AE, DC, V. Closed Sun. Métro: Étoile.*

$$ ✕ **La Fermette Marbeuf.** It's a favorite haunt of French TV and movie stars who like the spectacular Belle Epoque mosaics and stained glass and appreciate the solid, updated classic cuisine. Try gâteau of chicken livers and sweetbreads, saddle of lamb with *choron* (a tomato-spiked bearnaise sauce), and bitter chocolate fondant. Prices here are exceptional, considering the quality of the food, the surroundings, and the neighborhood. La Fermette becomes animated around 9 PM. ⊠ *5 rue Marbeuf,* ☎ *01–53–23–08–00. AE, DC, MC, V. Métro: Franklin-D.-Roosevelt.*

$$ ✕ **Sébillon.** The original Sébillon has nurtured chic residents of the fashionable suburb of Neuilly for generations; this elegant, polished branch off the Champs-Élysées continues the tradition. The menu includes lobster salad, lots of shellfish, and—the specialty—roast leg of lamb sliced tableside and served in unlimited quantity. Service is notably friendly. ⊠ *66 rue Pierre Charron,* ☎ *01–43–59–28–15. AE, DC, MC, V. Métro: Franklin-D.-Roosevelt.*

## 9ᵉ Arrondissement (Opéra)

FRENCH

$ ✕ **Chartier.** People come to this cavernous turn-of-the-century restaurant more for the bonhomie than the food, which is often rather ordinary. You may find yourself sharing a table as you study the long, old-fashioned menu of such favorites as steak tartare and roast chicken with fries. ✉ *7 rue du Faubourg-Montmartre,* ☎ *01–47–70–86–29. Reservations not accepted. No credit cards. Métro: Rue Montmartre.*

## 10ᵉ Arrondissement (République/ Gare du Nord)

FRENCH

**$$** ✕ **Brasserie Flo.** Though it's hard to find—down a passageway near Gare de l'Est—it's worth the effort. The rich wood and stained glass are typically Alsatian, service is enthusiastic, and brasserie standards such as shellfish and *choucroute* (sauerkraut and sausage) are savory. It's open until 1:30 AM, with a special night-owl menu from 11 PM. ✉ *7 cour des Petites Écuries,* ☎ *01–47–70–13–59. AE, DC, MC, V. Métro: Château d'Eau.*

**$–$$** ✕ **Chez Michel.** Chef Thierry Breton pulls a stylish crowd—despite the drab decor and neighborhood—with his wonderful cuisine du marché and dishes from his native Brittany. Typical of Breton's kitchen are the lasagna stuffed with chèvre and the artichokes and tuna steak with pureed peas. ✉ *10 rue Belzunce,* ☎ *01–44–53–06–20. Reservations essential. MC, V. Closed Sun.–Mon. No lunch Sat. Métro: Gare du Nord.*

## 11ᵉ Arrondissement (Bastille/République)

FRENCH

**$$** ✕ **Chardenoux.** A bit off the beaten path but well worth the effort, this cozy neighborhood bistro with etched-glass windows and a long zinc bar attracts a cross section of savvy Parisians. The traditional cooking is first-rate: delicious salads, game dishes, and savory desserts, with a nicely chosen wine list. ✉ *1 rue Jules-Valles,* ☎ *01–43–71–49–52. AE, V. Closed weekends and Aug. Métro: Charonne.*

**$$** ✕ **Le Repaire de Cartouche.** Near the Cirque d'Hiver, in the ★ Bastille, this split-level, '50s-style bistro with dark wood decor is the latest good-value bistro sensation in Paris. Young chef Rodolphe Paquin is a creative and impeccably trained cook who does a stylish take on earthy French regional dishes. The wine list is excellent, with bargains like a Pernand-Vergelesses (red Burgundy) for $20. ✉ *99 rue Amelot,* ☎ *01–47–00–25–86. AE, MC, V. Reservations essential. Closed Sun. No dinner Mon. Métro: Filles du Calvaire.*

**$** ✕ **Astier.** The prix-fixe menu (there's no à la carte) at this
pleasant restaurant is a remarkable value. Among the high-
quality seasonal dishes are baked eggs topped with truffled
foie gras, fricassee of *joue de boeuf* (beef cheeks), and plum
*clafoutis* (a creamy cake). Service can be rushed, but the
enthusiastic crowd does not seem to mind. Study the excellent wine list, which has some surprising buys. ⊠ *44 rue
Jean-Pierre Timbaud,* ☎ *01–43–57–16–35. AE, MC, V.
Closed weekends and Aug. Métro: Parmentier.*

**$** ✕ **Au Camelot.** This minuscule bistro with a single, five-
course menu brings in the crowds who come for the excellent
home-style cooking. A meal here usually begins with a
generous serving of soup, followed by a fish course, a main
dish, cheese, and dessert. Along with well-prepared classics, expect creative dishes like crab lasagna alongside classics like chicken in mushroom cream sauce. Though the place
is noisy and very crowded, service is friendly, and the house
Bordeaux is a treat. ⊠ *50 rue Amelot,* ☎ *01–43–55–54–
04. Reservations essential. No credit cards. Closed Sun. No
lunch Mon., Sat. Métro: République.*

## 12ᵉ Arrondissement (Bastille/Gare de Lyon)
FRENCH

**$$$** ✕ **Au Trou Gascon.** At this successful Belle Epoque estab-
lishment off Place Daumesnil, owner Alain Dutournier
serves his version of the cuisine of Gascony—a region of
outstanding ham, foie gras, lamb, and poultry—and his now-
classic white-chocolate mousse. ⊠ *40 rue Taine,* ☎ *01–43–
44–34–26. AE, DC, MC, V. Closed Sun., Christmas wk,
and Aug. No lunch Sat. Métro: Daumesnil.*

**$$** ✕ **Le Square Trousseau.** Since fashion designer Jean-Paul
Gaultier moved his headquarters nearby, this charming
turn-of-the-century bistro has become very chic. You might
see a supermodel or two while dining on the homemade
foie gras and tender baby chicken with mustard and bread-
crumb crust. The house wine is a good value, especially the
fruity red Morgon. ⊠ *1 rue Antoine Vollon,* ☎ *01–43–44–
06–00. MC, V. Métro: Ledru-Rollin.*

## 13ᵉ Arrondissement (Les Gobelins)
FRENCH

**$$** ✕ **Anacréon.** A former chef from the Tour d'Argent has
transformed a neighborhood café into a pleasant new-

# In case you want to see the world.

At American Express, we're here to make your journey
a smooth one. So we have over 1,700 travel service locations in over 130 countries ready to help. What else
would you expect from the world's largest travel agency?

do more  **Travel**

# In case you want to
# be welcomed there.

**We're here to see that you're always welcomed at establishments everywhere. That's why millions of people carry the American Express® Card – for peace of mind, confidence, and security, around the world or just around the corner.**

do more  AMERICAN EXPRESS

# In case you're running low.

We're here to help with more than 190,000 Express Cash locations around the world. In order to enroll, just call American Express at 1 800 CASH-NOW before you start your vacation.

do more

**Express Cash**

# And in case you'd rather be safe than sorry.

We're here with American Express® Travelers Cheques. They're the safe way to carry money on your vacation, because if they're ever lost or stolen you can get a refund, practically anywhere or anytime. To find the nearest place to buy Travelers Cheques, call 1 800 495-1153. Another way we help you do more.

*do more*® AMERICAN EXPRESS

**Travelers Cheques**

wave bistro. Inventive dishes such as compressed duck with red peppercorns, and fresh cod with spices have been highlights on the regularly changing menu. Desserts are always good, too, and the St-Joseph is a perfect choice from the wine list. ⊠ *53 bd. St-Marcel,* ☎ *01–43–31–71–18. Reservations essential. MC, V. Closed weekends. Métro: Les Gobelins.*

$ ✕ **Le Terroir.** A jolly crowd of regulars makes this little bistro festive. The solidly classical menu, based on first-rate ingredients from all over France, includes salads with chicken livers or fresh marinated anchovies, calves' liver or monkfish with saffron, and pears marinated in wine. ⊠ *11 bd. Arago,* ☎ *01–47–07–36–99. Closed Sun. No lunch Sat. Métro: Les Gobelins.*

## 14e Arrondissement (Montparnasse)
FRENCH

$$ ✕ **Contre-Allée.** Students and professors crowd this large restaurant, simply decorated with bullfighting posters. The menu has selections such as squid salad with mussels and roast cod with Parmesan; homemade pasta accompanies many dishes. A sidewalk terrace enlivens shady avenue Denfert-Rochereau in summer. The restaurant serves until 11:30 PM. ⊠ *83 av. Denfert-Rochereau,* ☎ *01–43–54–99–86. AE, DC, MC, V. No lunch Sat. Métro: Denfert-Rochereau.*

$$ ✕ **La Coupole.** This world-renowned, cavernous address in Montparnasse practically defines the term brasserie (it's owned by Jean-Paul Bucher)—and its murals are famous, too. Many find it too large, too noisy, and too expensive, and no one likes the long wait at the bar before being seated. Still, it has been popular with everyone from Left Bank intellectuals (Jean-Paul Sartre and Simone de Beauvoir were regulars) to bourgeois grandmothers. Expect the usual brasserie menu, including perhaps the largest shellfish presentation in Paris, choucroute, and a wide range of desserts. ⊠ *102 bd. du Montparnasse,* ☎ *01–43–20–14–20. AE, DC, MC, V. Métro: Vavin.*

## 15e Arrondissement (Motte-Picquet/Balard)
FRENCH

$$ ✕ **Bistrot d'Hubert.** In a studied environment that might have sprung from the pages of *Elle Décor,* this popular bistro—

frequented by a stylish crowd—serves food that perfectly expresses the countercurrents of the Parisian culinary landscape. The prix-fixe menu is split into two: "tradition" and "innovation." You might have the tuna steak in a "caramel" of balsamic vinegar, or go for the more classic roast lamb. ⊠ *41 bd. Pasteur,* ☎ *01–47–34–15–50. Reservations essential. AE, DC, MC, V. Métro: Pasteur.*

**$$** ✕ **Philippe Detourbe.** Amid black lacquer, mirrors, and
★ burgundy velvet upholstery, sample Detourbe's spectacular contemporary French cooking. The menu changes with every meal and may include smoked salmon filled with cabbage *rémoulade* (cabbage in a creamy dressing) or cod steak with white beans and caramelized endives; desserts are fantastic. The wine list is brief but well chosen; service is friendly and efficient. ⊠ *8 rue Nicolas Charlet,* ☎ *01–42–19–08–59. Reservations essential. MC, V. Closed Sun. No lunch Sat. Métro: Pasteur.*

## 16ᵉ Arrondissement (Arc de Triomphe)
FRENCH

**$$$$** ✕ **Alain Ducasse.** Since he took over from Joël Robuchon, Ducasse has surprised everyone by serving resolutely classical French dishes. Ducasse is a marvelous cook, but his creativity is lost on traditional dishes. Other dishes, though, like the duckling roasted with fig leaves, show his brilliant subtlety. Be forewarned that service is snippy and the food staggeringly expensive; the 480-franc lunch menu is your best bet. ⊠ *59 av. Raymond-Poincaré,* ☎ *01–47–27–12–27. Reservations several months in advance essential. AE, DC, MC, V. Closed weekends. Métro: Victor Hugo.*

**$$$** ✕ **Jamin.** At this intimate, elegant restaurant, where Joël
★ Robuchon made his name, you can find excellent haute cuisine at almost half the price of what you'd find elsewhere. Benoit Guichard, Robuchon's second for many years, is a subtle and accomplished chef and a particularly brilliant *saucier* (sauce maker). The menu changes regularly, but Guichard tends toward dishes like sea bass with pistachios in fennel sauce, and braised beef with cumin-scented carrots. The gratin of rhubarb with a red-fruit sauce makes an excellent dessert. ⊠ *32 rue de Longchamp,* ☎ *01–45–53–00–07. Reservations essential. AE, DC, MC, V. Closed Sun. No lunch Sat. Métro: Iéna.*

**$$–$$$** ✕ **Prunier.** Founded in 1925, this seafood restaurant is one of the best—and the prettiest—in Paris. The famous Art Deco mosaics glitter, and the white marble counters shine with impeccably fresh shellfish. The kitchen not only excels at classic French fish dishes but has added some interesting options, like a *Saintongeaise* plate—raw oysters with grilled sausages. ✉ *16 av. Victor-Hugo,* ☎ *01–44–17–35–85. Reservations essential in upstairs dining room. Jacket and tie. AE, DC, MC, V. Closed Sun.–Mon. Métro: Charles-de-Gaulle–Étoile.*

**$$** ✕ **La Butte Chaillot.** A dramatic iron staircase connects two levels in turquoise and earth tones at one of the most popular of chef Guy Savoy's fashionable bistros. Dining here is part theater, as the à la mode clientele demonstrate, but it's not all show: The very good food includes tasty ravioli from the town of Royans, roast chicken with mashed potatoes, and stuffed veal breast with rosemary. A wide sidewalk terrace fronts tree-shaded avenue Kléber. ✉ *112 av. Kléber,* ☎ *01–47–27–88–88. AE, MC, V. Métro: Trocadéro.*

**$$** ✕ **Le Relais du Parc.** This bistro-annex is the place to try a lighter version of Alain Ducasse's cooking for less. Two delicious starters—the lobster salad, and the baby potatoes with black truffles in a creamy oxtail-stock sauce—make good meals, followed by cheese or dessert. Main courses are also excellent, but the desserts could be better, and wine is overpriced. ✉ *55 av. Raymond-Poincaré,* ☎ *01–44–05–66–10. Reservations essential. AE, DC, MC, V. Métro: Victor Hugo.*

**$** ✕ **Les Chauffeurs.** Not only is this tranquil bistro in this expensive part of town a favorite address of well-dressed regulars, but it's also the night-off hangout for some of the capital's best-known chefs. What attracts the discerning and the experts is the moderately priced, reliably good classic cooking and the pleasant, relaxed ambience. Try the airy fish terrine or an Alsatian *cervelas* (fine pork sausage) salad, and then, depending on what's on the menu, go for the sole meunière or the roast chicken. Good Beaujolais wines are served by the carafe. *8 chaussée de la Muette,* ☎ *01–42–88–50–05. MC, V. Métro: La Muette.*

**$** ✕ **Le Petit Rétro.** Two types of clientele—men in expensive suits at noon and well-dressed couples in the evening—frequent this little bistro with Art Nouveau tiles and bentwood furniture. You can't go wrong with the daily special writ-

ten on the chalkboard. Come when you want a good solid
meal, like the perfect *pavé de boeuf* (thick steak). ⊠ *5 rue
Mesnil,* ☎ *01–44–05–06–05. MC, V. Closed Sun. No lunch
Mon. Métro: Victor Hugo.*

## 17ᵉ Arrondissement (Monceau/Clichy)

FRENCH

**$$$$**   ✕ **Guy Savoy.** Top chef Guy Savoy's other five bistros have
not distracted him too much from his handsome luxury
restaurant near the Arc de Triomphe. The oysters in aspic
and grilled pigeon reveal the magnitude of his talent, and
the mille-feuille is a contemporary classic. ⊠ *18 rue Troyon,*
☎ *01–43–80–40–61. Reservations essential. AE, MC, V.
Closed Sun. No lunch Sat. Métro: Charles-de-Gaulle–Étoile.*

NORTH AFRICAN

**$$**   ✕ **Le Timgad.** For a stylish evening out and a night off from
French food, try this elegant North African restaurant.
Start with a savory *brick* (crispy parchment pastry filled with
meat, eggs, or seafood), followed by tasty couscous or suc-
culent *tagine* (meat or poultry that's slowly braised inside
a domed pottery casserole). ⊠ *21 rue de Brunel,* ☎ *01–
45–74–23–70. MC, V. Métro: Argentine.*

## 18ᵉ Arrondissement (Montmartre)

FRENCH

**$**   ✕ **Le Moulin à Vins.** The atmosphere at this popular wine
bar–bistro is sepia toned—both it and the surrounding
neighborhood evoke old Paris. It's perfect for lunch while
touring Montmartre. In the evening it's livelier, when de-
voted regulars come for the daily short list of hot dishes.
⊠ *6 rue Burq,* ☎ *01–45–52–81–27. MC, V. Closed Mon.
Métro: Abbesses.*

## 19ᵉ Arrondissement (Buttes Chaumont/ La Villette)

FRENCH

**$$**   ✕ **Le Restaurant d'Eric Frechon.** This simple little spot is a
★   sterling example of a price-conscious, market-menu bistro.
Chef Frechon worked with Christian Constant at the Hôtel
Crillon (☞ Chapter 4), which means his cooking is more
adventurous and elegant than most other bistro fare. ⊠ *10
rue du Général-Brunet,* ☎ *01–40–40–03–30. V. Closed
weekends. Métro: Danube.*

# Cafés and Salons de Thé

Cafés can be found at every bend in Paris; following is a small selection of cafés and *salons de thé* (tearooms) to whet your appetite. **Au Père Tranquille** (⊠ 16 rue Pierre Lescot, 1ᵉʳ, ☎ 01–45–08–00–34, métro Les Halles) is one of the best places in Paris for people-watching. **Café Beaubourg** (⊠ 43 rue St-Merri, 4ᵉ, ☎ 01–48–87–63–96, métro Hôtel-de-Ville), near the Pompidou Center, is a slick, modern spot. **Café Marly** (⊠ Cour Napoléon du Louvre, 93 rue de Rivoli, 1ᵉʳ, ☎ 01–49–26–06–60, métro Palais-Royal), overlooking the main courtyard of the Louvre, is perfect for an afternoon break or a nightcap. **La Crémaillère** (⊠ 15 Pl. du Tertre, 18ᵉ, ☎ 01–46–06–58–59, métro Anvers) is a veritable monument to fin-de-siècle art in Montmartre. **Ma Bourgogne** (⊠ 19 Pl. des Vosges, 4ᵉ, ☎ 01–42–78–44–64, métro St-Paul) is a calm oasis for a coffee or a light lunch away from the noisy streets. **Mariage Frères** (⊠ 30 rue du Bourg-Tibourg, 4ᵉ, ☎ 01–42–72–28–11, métro Hôtel-de-Ville) is an outstanding tea shop serving 500 kinds of tea, along with delicious tarts. **Salon de Thé du Palais Royal** (⊠ Jardins du Palais Royal, 110 Galérie de Valois, 1ᵉʳ, ☎ 01–40–20–00–27, métro Palais-Royal) serves tea on a terrace overlooking the gardens of the Palais Royal. **Le Vieux Colombier** (⊠ 65 rue de Rennes, 7ᵉ, ☎ 01–45–48–53–81, métro St-Sulpice) is just around the corner from St-Sulpice and the Vieux Colombier Theater.

# Wine Bars

Wine bars are a good place to sample a glass (or bottle) of French wine and have an excellent, simple hot meal or just a plate of cheese or charcuterie. Hours can vary widely, so it's best to check ahead; many close around 10 PM. **Aux Bons Crus** (⊠ 7 rue des Petits-Champs, 1ᵉʳ, ☎ 01–42–60–06–45, métro Bourse) is a cramped, narrow venue with an authentically Parisian feel. **Le Baron Rouge** (⊠ 1 rue Théophile-Roussel, 12ᵉ, ☎ 01–43–43–14–32, métro Ledru-Rollin) is a noisy and convivial haunt. **Jacques Mélac** (⊠ 42 rue Léon-Frot, 11ᵉ, ☎ 01–43–70–59–27, métro Charonne) is named after the jolly owner who bottles several of his own wines—try the chewy red Lirac.

# 4 Lodging

Revised
and
updated by
Christopher
Mooney

**W**INDING STAIRCASES, flower-filled window boxes, concierges who seem to have stepped from a 19th-century novel—all of these still exist in Paris hotels. So do grand rooms with marble baths, Belle Epoque lobbies, and polished staff at your beck and call. In Paris there are wonderful hotels for every taste and budget.

Our criteria when selecting the hotels reviewed below were quality, location, and character. Fewer hotels are listed in outlying arrondissements (the 10$^e$ to the 20$^e$) because these are farther from the major sights. Generally, there are more hotels on the Right Bank offering luxury—or at any rate formality—than there are on the Left Bank, where hotels are frequently smaller and richer in old-fashioned ambience. In Paris's oldest quarters hotel rooms are generally much smaller than their American counterparts. Although air-conditioning has become de rigueur in middle- to higher-price hotels, it is generally not a prerequisite for comfort (Paris's hot weather season doesn't usually last long).

Despite the huge choice of hotels, you should always reserve well in advance, especially if you're determined to stay in a specific place. You can do this by telephoning or faxing ahead, then asking for written or faxed confirmation of your reservation, detailing the duration of your stay, the price, the location and type of your room (single or double, twin beds or double), and the bathroom (shower—*douche,* or bath—*baignoire,* private or shared).

Almost all Paris hotels charge extra for breakfast, with prices ranging from 30 francs to more than 200 francs per person in luxury establishments. For anything more than the standard Continental breakfast of café au lait and croissants, the price will be higher. You may be better off finding the nearest café. A nominal *séjour* (lodging) tax of 7 francs per person, per night is charged to pay for promotion of tourism in Paris.

| CATEGORY | COST* |
|---|---|
| **$$$$** | over 1750 frs |
| **$$$** | 1000 frs–1750 frs |
| **$$** | 600 frs–1000 frs |
| **$** | under 600 frs |

*All prices are for a standard double room, including 20.6% tax and service.*

# 1er Arrondissement (Louvre/Les Halles)

**$$$$**   🏨 **Costes.** Jean-Louis and Gilbert Costes's sumptuous hotel
★    is the darling of the fashion and media set. Conjuring up the
palaces of Napoléon III, rooms are swathed in rich garnet
and bronze tones and contain a luxurious mélange of patterned fabrics, heavy swags, and enough brocade and fringe
to blanket the Champs-Élysées. ✉ *239 rue St-Honoré, 75001,*
☎ *01-42-44-50-50, ғᴀх 01-42-44-50-01. 85 rooms. Restaurant, bar, air-conditioning, in-room data ports, in-room safes,
room service, indoor pool, sauna, exercise room, laundry service. AE, DC, MC, V. Métro:Tuileries.*

**$$$$**   🏨 **Meurice.** The Meurice, owned by the Audrey group, is
one of the finest hotels in the city. The Louis XVI–style first-
floor salons are luxurious and the bedrooms, adorned with
Persian carpets, opulent. Book well in advance to land a
room or a suite overlooking the Tuileries Garden. The
hotel's restaurant is fabled. ✉ *228 rue de Rivoli, 75001,*
☎ *01-44-58-10-10, ғᴀх 01-44-58-10-15. 180 rooms,
28 suites. Restaurant, bar, air-conditioning, no-smoking
rooms, room service, laundry service, business services.
AE, DC, MC, V. Métro:Tuileries, Concorde.*

**$$$$**   🏨 **Ritz.** The Ritz is the crowning gem of sparkling Place
Vendôme. Festooned with gilt and ormolu, dripping with
crystal chandeliers, and swathed in heavy silk and tapestries,
this hotel, which opened in 1896, is the epitome of fin-de-
siècle Paris. Yet it's surprisingly intimate. Don't miss the
famous Hemingway Bar (which the writer claimed to have
"liberated" in 1944). ✉ *15 Pl. Vendôme, 75001, ☎ 01–
43-16-30-30, ғᴀх 01-43-16-36-68. 142 rooms, 45 suites.
3 restaurants, 2 bars, air-conditioning, in-room safes, room
service, indoor pool, beauty salon, health club, shops, laundry service, meeting rooms, parking (fee). AE, DC, MC, V.
Métro:Opéra.*

$$$–$$$$  ☒ **Vendôme.** This hotel has the best guest-to-staff ratio in
★ Paris and every luxury perk imaginable. Rooms are in
sumptuous, Second Empire style and bathrooms are over
the top. Best of all, besides a videophone for checking out
visitors at the door, is the fully automated bedside console
that controls the lights, curtains, and electronic do-not-dis-
turb sign. ⊠ *1 Pl. Vendôme, 75001,* ☎ *01–42–60–32–84,*
FAX *01–49–27–97–89. 19 rooms, 11 suites. Restaurant, bar,
air-conditioning, room service, baby-sitting, in-room safes,
in-room modem lines, laundry service. AE, DC, MC, V.
Métro:Concorde, Opéra.*

$$  ☒ **Britannique.** Open since 1870, the Britannique blends
courteous English service with old-fashioned French elegance.
It has retained its handsome winding staircase and has
well-appointed, soundproof rooms in chic, warm tones. ⊠
*20 av. Victoria, 75001,* ☎ *01–42–33–74–59,* FAX *01–42–
33–82–65. 40 rooms. Bar, in-room safes. AE, DC, MC, V.
Métro:Châtelet.*

$  ☒ **Louvre Forum.** This hotel is a find:Smack in the center
★ of town, it has a friendly feel and clean, comfortable, well-
equipped rooms (minibars, satellite TV). ⊠ *25 rue du
Bouloi, 75001,* ☎ *01–42–36–54–19,* FAX *01–42–33–66–31.
27 rooms. Bar, minibars. AE, DC, MC, V. Métro:Louvre.*

## 2ᵉ Arrondissement (La Bourse)

$$  ☒ **Grand Hôtel de Besançon.** This terrific hotel, with its very
Parisian cream-colored facade and wrought-iron balconies,
has it all—intimacy, comfort, affordability, and a location
on a delightful, pedestrian market street near Les Halles,
the Pompidou Center, and the Marais. Rooms are classi-
cally decorated with French upholsteries and period re-
productions, and despite the busy area nearby, they are quiet.
⊠ *56 rue Montorgueil, 75002,* ☎ *01–42–36–41–08,* FAX *01–
45–08–08–79. 11 rooms, 14 suites. In-room modem lines,
in-room safes, laundry service. AE, DC, MC, V. Métro:Eti-
enne-Marcel, Les Halles.*

$$  ☒ **Hôtel de Noailles.** With a nod to the work of postmodern designers like Putman and Starck, this new-wave inn
(part of the Tulip Inn group) is a star among Paris's new
crop of well-priced, style-driven boutique hotels. Though
not to everyone's taste, rooms are imaginatively decorated

# Paris Lodging

L'Astor, **5**

Atelier
Montparnasse, **28**

Bretonnerie, **16**

Britannique, **33**

Caron de
Beaumarchais, **17**

Castex, **21**

Costes, **8**

Deux-Iles, **20**

Étoile-Péreire, **3**

Familia, **23**

Grand Hôtel de
Besançon, **15**

Grand Hôtel
Inter-
Continental, **12**

Grandes
Écoles, **24**

Hôtel
d'Aubusson, **32**

Hôtel Crillon, **7**

Hôtel de
L'Abbaye, **29**

Hôtel de
Noailles, **13**

Hôtel du
7e Art, **19**

Hyatt Regency
Paris–
Madeleine, **6**

Jardin du
Luxembourg, **25**

Lancaster, **4**

Latour
Maubourg, **35**

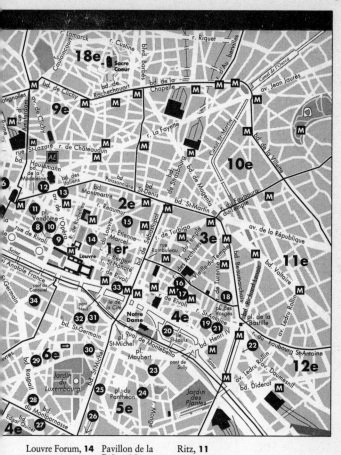

Louvre Forum, **14**
Meurice, **9**
Montalem-
bert, **34**
Parc
Montsouris, **26**
Le Pavillon
Bastille, **22**

Pavillon de la
Reine, **18**
Queen's Hotel, **1**
Raspail-
Montparnasse, **27**
Relais
Christine, **31**
Relais
St-Germain, **30**

Ritz, **11**
Saint James
Paris, **2**
Le Tourville, **36**
Vendôme, **10**

with funky furnishings and contemporary details. ⊠ *9 rue de Michodière, 75002,* ☎ *01–47–42–92–90,* ℻ *01–49–24–92–71. 58 rooms. Bar, air-conditioning, laundry service. AE, DC, MC, V. Métro:Opéra.*

## 3ᵉ Arrondissement (Beaubourg/Marais)

**$$$$** 🏨 **Pavillon de la Reine.** On lovely Place des Vosges, this magnificent mansion, reconstructed from original plans, is filled with Louis XIII–style fireplaces and antiques. Ask for a duplex with French windows overlooking the first of two flower-filled courtyards behind the historic Queen's Pavilion. ⊠ *28 Pl. des Vosges, 75003,* ☎ *01–40–29–19–19; 800/447–7462 in the U.S.,* ℻ *01–40–29–19–20. 30 rooms, 25 suites. Bar, breakfast room, air-conditioning, room service, laundry service, free parking. AE, DC, MC, V. Métro:Bastille, St-Paul.*

## 4ᵉ Arrondissement (Marais/Ile St-Louis)

**$$** 🏨 **Bretonnerie.** This small hotel is in a 17th-century *hôtel particulier* (town house) on a tiny street in the Marais, a few minutes' walk from the Pompidou Center. Rooms are done in Louis XIII style, complete with upholstered walls; they vary considerably in size from spacious to cramped. ⊠ *22 rue Ste-Croix-de-la-Bretonnerie, 75004,* ☎ *01–48–87–77–63,* ℻ *01–42–77–26–78. 27 rooms, 3 suites. In-room safes. MC, V. Métro:Hôtel de Ville.*

**$$** 🏨 **Caron de Beaumarchais.** The theme of this intimate
★ jewel is the work of Caron de Beaumarchais, who wrote *The Marriage of Figaro* in 1778. Rooms faithfully reflect the taste of 18th-century French nobility. The second- and fifth-floor rooms with balconies are the largest; those on the sixth floor have beguiling views across Right Bank rooftops. ⊠ *12 rue Vieille-du-Temple, 75004,* ☎ *01–42–72–34–12,* ℻ *01–42–72–34–63. 19 rooms. Air-conditioning, in-room safes, laundry service. AE, DC, MC, V. Métro:Hôtel de Ville.*

**$$** 🏨 **Deux-Iles.** This converted 17th-century mansion on the Ile St-Louis has long won plaudits for charm and comfort. The delightfully old-fashioned rooms, blessed with exposed beams, are small but airy; ask for one overlooking the little garden courtyard. In winter a roaring fire warms the lounge. ⊠ *59 rue St-Louis-en-l'Ile, 75004,* ☎ *01–43–26–13–35,* ℻ *01–43–29–60–25. 17 rooms. Air-conditioning, in-room safes, baby-sitting. AE, MC, V. Métro:Pont-Marie.*

**$–$$** 🏨 **Hôtel du 7ᵉ Art.** The theme of this hip Marais hotel ("Seventh Art" is what the French call filmmaking) is Hollywood from the '40s to the '60s. Rooms are small and spartan but clean, quiet, and equipped with cable TV. There's no elevator, but there is a pleasant bar. The clientele is young, trendy, and primarily American. ⊠ *20 rue St-Paul, 75004,* ☎ *01–44–54–85–00,* ℻ *01–42–77–69–10. 23 rooms. Bar, in-room safes. AE, DC, MC, V. Métro:St-Paul.*

**$** 🏨 **Castex.** This Marais hotel in a Revolution-era building is a bargain hunter's dream. Rooms are low on frills but squeaky clean and up to date, the owners are extremely friendly, and the prices are rock bottom, which ensures the hotel is often booked months ahead. There's no elevator, and the only TV is in the ground-floor salon. ⊠ *5 rue Castex, 75004,* ☎ *01–42–72–31–52,* ℻ *01–42–72–57–91. 27 rooms, 23 with shower. MC, V. Métro:Bastille.*

# 5ᵉ Arrondissement (Latin Quarter)

**$$$** 🏨 **Jardin du Luxembourg.** Blessed with a charming staff and a stylish look, this hotel is one of the most sought after in the Latin Quarter. Rooms are a bit small (common for this neighborhood) but intelligently furnished for optimal space and warmly decorated in ocher, rust, and indigo *à la provençale.* Ask for one with a balcony overlooking the street; the best, No. 25, has a peekaboo view of the Eiffel Tower. ⊠ *5 impasse Royer-Collard, 75005,* ☎ *01–40–46–08–88,* ℻ *01–40–46–02–28. 27 rooms. Air-conditioning, in-room safes, no-smoking rooms, sauna. AE, DC, MC, V. Métro:Luxembourg.*

**$** 🏨 **Familia.** The hospitable Gaucheron family, the owners,
★ bends over backward for you. About half the rooms feature romantic sepia frescoes of celebrated Paris scenes; others are appointed with exquisite Louis XV–style furnishings or have nice mahogany pieces. Book a month ahead for one with a walk-out balcony on the second or fifth floor. ⊠ *11 rue des Écoles, 75005,* ☎ *01–43–54–55–27,* ℻ *01–43–29–61–77. 30 rooms. AE, MC, V. Métro:Cardinal Lemoine.*

**$** 🏨 **Grandes Écoles.** This delightfully intimate place looks and feels like a country cottage dropped smack in the middle of the Latin Quarter. It's off the street and occupies three buildings on a beautiful leafy garden. Parquet floors, Louis-Philippe furnishings, lace bedspreads, and the absence of TV all add to the rustic ambience. ✉ *75 rue du Cardinal Lemoine, 75005,* ☎ *01–43–26–79–23,* 📠 *01–43–25–28–15. 51 rooms. Parking (fee). MC, V. Métro:Cardinal Lemoine.*

## 6ᵉ Arrondissement (St-Germain/Montparnasse)

**$$$$** 🏨 **Relais Christine.** On a quiet street between the Seine and boulevard St-Germain, this luxurious and popular hotel, occupying 16th-century abbey cloisters, oozes romantic ambience. Rooms are spacious (particularly the duplexes on the upper floors) and well appointed in old Parisian style; the best have exposed beams and overlook the garden. ✉ *3 rue Christine, 75006,* ☎ *01–40–51–60–80; 800/447–7462 in the U.S.,* 📠 *01–40–51–60–81. 31 rooms, 18 suites. Bar, air-conditioning, no-smoking rooms, room service, baby-sitting, laundry service, meeting rooms, free parking. AE, DC, MC, V. Métro:Odéon.*

**$$$$** 🏨 **Relais St-Germain.** The interior-designer owners of this
★ outstanding hotel have exquisite taste and a superb respect for tradition and detail. Moreover, the rooms are at least twice the size of those in other hotels in the area for the same price. Much of the furniture was selected with a knowledgeable eye from the city's *brocantes* (secondhand dealers), and every room has unique treasures. Breakfast is included. ✉ *9 carrefour de l'Odéon, 75006,* ☎ *01–43–29–12–05,* 📠 *01–46–33–45–30. 21 rooms, 1 suite. AE, DC, MC, V. Métro:Odéon.*

**$$$** 🏨 **Hôtel de L'Abbaye.** This delightful hotel near St-Sulpice was transformed from an erstwhile convent. The blend of stylishly rustic antiques and earthy apricot and ocher tones makes for a calm, cozy atmosphere. The first-floor rooms open onto the garden; most of those on the upper floors have oak beams and sitting alcoves. The four duplexes with private terraces are more expensive. Breakfast is included. ✉ *10 rue Cassette, 75006,* ☎ *01–45–44–38–11,* 📠 *01–45–48–07–86. 42 rooms, 4 suites. Bar, air-condi-*

*tioning, room service, baby-sitting, laundry service. AE, MC, V. Métro:St-Sulpice.*

**$$–$$$**   ⊞ **Hôtel d'Aubusson.** This good-value hotel keeps prices
★   in check while offering original Aubusson tapestries, Versailles-style parquet floors, a chiseled stone fireplace, and restored antiques. Even the smallest rooms are a good size by Paris standards, and all are decked out in rich burgundies, greens, or blues. The 10 best rooms have canopied beds and ceiling beams. ⊠ *33 rue Dauphine, 75006,* ☎ *01–43–29–43–43,* 🗏 *01–43–29–12–62. 49 rooms. Bar, air-conditioning, in-room safes, baby-sitting, laundry service. AE, MC, V. Métro:Odéon.*

**$$**   ⊞ **Atelier Montparnasse.** This Art Deco–inspired gem of a hotel was designed with style and comfort in mind. Rooms are tastefully decorated and spacious, and all the bathrooms feature mosaic reproductions of famous French paintings. One of the rooms sleeps three. The hotel is within walking distance of the Luxembourg Garden and St-Germain-des-Prés. ⊠ *49 rue Vavin, 75006,* ☎ *01–46–33–60–00,* 🗏 *01–40–51–04–21. 17 rooms. Bar, room service, baby-sitting, laundry service. AE, DC, MC, V. Métro:Vavin.*

# 7ᵉ Arrondissement (Invalides/École Militaire)

**$$$$**   ⊞ **Montalembert.** This place is one of Paris's most originally voguish boutique hotels. Whether appointed with traditional or contemporary furnishings, rooms are all about simple lines and chic luxury. Ask about special packages if you're staying for more than three nights. ⊠ *3 rue de Montalembert, 75007,* ☎ *01–45–49–68–68; 800/628–8929 in the U.S.,* 🗏 *01–45–49–69–49. 50 rooms, 6 suites. Restaurant, bar, air-conditioning, in-room data ports, in-room safes, room service, in-room VCRs, baby-sitting, meeting rooms. AE, DC, MC, V. Métro:Rue du Bac.*

**$$–$$$**   ⊞ **Le Tourville.** Here is a rare find: an intimate, upscale
★   hotel at an affordable price. Each room has crisp, virginwhite damask upholstery set against pastel or ocher walls, a smattering of antiques, original artwork, and fabulous old mirrors. The staff couldn't be more helpful. ⊠ *16 av. de Tourville, 75007,* ☎ *01–47–05–62–62; 800/528–3549*

*in the U.S.,* FAX *01–47–05–43–90. 27 rooms, 3 junior suites. Bar, air-conditioning, laundry service. AE, DC, MC, V. Métro:École Militaire.*

**$$**    🏨 **Latour Maubourg.** In the residential heart of the ritzy seventh, a stone's throw from Invalides, this hotel with a friendly staff has been inked into many a traveler's journal. Decor is homey and unpretentious, and with just 10 rooms, the accent is on intimacy and personalized service. ⊠ *150 rue de Grenelle, 75007,* ☎ *01–47–05–16–16,* FAX *01–47–05–16–14. 9 rooms, 1 suite. In-room safes. MC, V. Métro:Latour Maubourg.*

## 8ᵉ Arrondissement (Champs-Élysées)

**$$$$**    🏨 **L'Astor.** Following a top-to-bottom makeover by the Westin-Demeure group, L'Astor has been reborn as a bastion of highly stylized, civilized chic. The lobby is Art Deco; rooms are testimonials to the sober Regency style, with weighty marble fireplaces and mahogany furnishings. The hotel's restaurant is supervised by the celebrated chef Joël Robuchon. ⊠ *11 rue d'Astorg, 75008,* ☎ *01–53–05–05–05; 800/937–8461 in the U.S.,* FAX *01–53–05–05–30. 134 rooms, 5 suites. Restaurant, bar, air-conditioning, in-room data ports, in-room safes, no-smoking rooms, room service, beauty salon, health club, laundry service. AE, DC, MC, V. Métro:Miromesnil, St-Augustin.*

**$$$$**    🏨 **Hôtel Crillon.** One of Paris's most famous palace hotels, the Crillon is in two 18th-century town houses on Place de la Concorde. Rooms are lavish, with rococo and Directoire furnishings and crystal and gilt wall sconces. The sheer quantity of marble downstairs—especially in Les Ambassadeurs restaurant—is staggering. ⊠ *10 Pl. de la Concorde, 75008,* ☎ *01–44–71–15–00; 800/888–4747 in the U.S.,* FAX *01–44–71–15–02. 118 rooms, 45 suites. 2 restaurants, 2 bars, tea shop, air-conditioning, in-room safes, no-smoking rooms, room service, exercise room, baby-sitting, laundry service, meeting rooms. AE, DC, MC, V. Métro:Concorde.*

**$$$$**    🏨 **Hyatt Regency Paris–Madeleine.** This stunning Haussmann-esque building near the Opéra Garnier feels more like a boutique hotel than an international business chain, thanks to stylized details like cherry paneling and mismatched bedside tables. Book a room on the seventh or eighth floor facing boulevard Malesherbes for a view of the Eiffel Tower. ✉ *24 bd. Malesherbes, 75008,* ☎ *01–55–27–12–34; 800/223–1234 in the U.S.,* FAX *01–55–27–12–35. 81 rooms, 5 suites. Restaurant, bar, air-conditioning, in-room data ports, in-room safes, no-smoking floors, room service, sauna, exercise room, laundry service, meeting rooms. AE, DC, MC, V. Métro:St-Augustin.*

**$$$$** 🏨 **Lancaster.** The Lancaster—one of Paris's most venerable
★    institutions, now owned by the Savoy group—has been meticulously transformed into one of the city's most modish luxury hotels. The clubby decor seamlessly blends the traditional with the contemporary to evoke an overall feeling of timeless elegance. ✉ *7 rue de Berri, 75008,* ☎ *01–40–76–40–76; 800/637–2869 in the U.S.,* FAX *01–40–76–40–00. 50 rooms, 10 suites. Restaurant, bar, air-conditioning, in-room data ports, in-room safes, room service, in-room VCRs, sauna, exercise room, baby-sitting, laundry service, meeting rooms. AE, DC, MC, V. Métro:George-V.*

## 9ᵉ Arrondissement (Opéra)

**$$$$** 🏨 **Grand Hôtel Inter-Continental.** Open since 1862, Paris's biggest luxury hotel has a facade that seems as long as the Louvre. The grand salon's Art Deco dome and the restaurant's painted ceilings are registered landmarks. The Art Deco rooms are spacious and light (ask for one on the top floors). Its famed Café de la Paix is one of the city's great people-watching spots. ✉ *2 rue Scribe, 75009,* ☎ *01–40–07–32–32; 800/327–0200 in the U.S.,* FAX *01–42–66–12–51. 475 rooms, 39 suites. 3 restaurants, 2 bars, air-conditioning, in-room data ports, in-room safes, no-smoking rooms, room service, in-room VCRs, sauna, health club, laundry service, business services, meeting rooms. AE, DC, MC, V. Métro:Opéra.*

## 12ᵉ Arrondissement (Bastille/Gare de Lyon)

**$$–$$$** 🏨 **Le Pavillon Bastille.** The transformation of this 19th-century *hôtel particulier* (across from the Opéra Bastille) into a mod, colorful, high-design hotel garnered architectural awards and a fiercely loyal, hip clientele. ✉ *65 rue de Lyon, 75012,* ☎ *01–43–43–65–65; 800/233–2552 in the U.S.,* FAX *01–43–43–96–52. 24 rooms, 1 suite. Bar, air-con-*

*ditioning, in-room safes, minibars, room service. AE, DC, MC, V. Métro:Bastille.*

## 14ᵉ Arrondissement (Montparnasse)

$$ ⊞ **Raspail-Montparnasse.** Rooms in this hotel are named after the artists who made Montparnasse the art capital of the world in the '20s and '30s. All are decorated in pastels and contemporary blond-wood furniture. Most are at the low end of this price category; five have spectacular panoramic views of Montparnasse and the Eiffel Tower. ⊠ *203 bd. Raspail, 75014,* ☎ *01–43–20–62–86,* ☎ *01–43–20–50–79. 38 rooms. Bar, air-conditioning, in-room safes, meeting rooms. AE, DC, MC, V. Métro:Vavin.*

$ ⊞ **Parc Montsouris.** This modest hotel in a 1930s villa is on a quiet residential street next to the lovely Parc Montsouris. Attractive oak pieces and high-quality French fabrics embellish the small but clean rooms; satellite TV is another plus. Those with shower are very inexpensive; suites sleep four. ⊠ *4 rue du Parc-Montsouris, 75014,* ☎ *01–45–89–09–72,* ☎ *01–45–80–92–72. 28 rooms, 7 suites. Air-conditioning, no-smoking rooms, laundry service. AE, MC, V. Métro:Montparnasse-Bienvenue.*

## 16ᵉ Arrondissement (Arc de Triomphe/Le Bois)

$$$$ ⊞ **Saint James Paris.** Called the "only château-hôtel in Paris," this gracious late-19th-century Neoclassical mansion is surrounded by a lush private park. The lavish Art Deco interior was created by designer Andrée Putman. Ten rooms on the third floor open onto a winter garden. The restaurant is reserved for guests; in warm weather meals are served in the garden. ⊠ *43 av. Bugeaud, 75016,* ☎ *01–44–05–81–81; 800/447–7462 in the U.S.,* ☎ *01–44–05–81–82. 24 rooms, 24 suites. Restaurant, bar, air-conditioning, in-room data ports, in-room safes, no-smoking rooms, room service, sauna, health club, baby-sitting, laundry service, meeting rooms, free parking. AE, DC, MC, V. Métro:Porte Dauphine.*

$ ⊞ **Queen's Hôtel.** One of only a handful of hotels in the tony residential district near the Bois de Boulogne, Queen's is a small, comfortable hotel with a high standard of service. Each room focuses on a different 20th-century French artist. The rooms with baths have Jacuzzis. ⊠ *4 rue Bastien-Lepage, 75016,* ☎ *01–42–88–89–85,* FAX *01–40–50–67–52. 22 rooms. Air-conditioning, in-room safes, no-smoking rooms. AE, DC, MC, V. Métro:Michel-Ange–Auteuil.*

## 17ᵉ Arrondissement (Monceau/Clichy)

$$ 🏨 **Étoile-Péreire.** Behind a quiet, leafy courtyard in this chic residential district is this unique, intimate hotel, consisting of two parts:a fin-de-siècle building on the street and a 1920s annex overlooking an interior courtyard. Rooms and duplexes are done in deep shades of rose or blue with crisp, white damask upholstery; only suites have air-conditioning. ⊠ *146 bd. Péreire, 75017,* ☎ *01–42–67–60–00,* FAX *01–42–67–02–90. 21 rooms, 5 duplex suites. Bar, in-room safes, no-smoking rooms, laundry service. AE, DC, MC, V. Métro:Péreire.*

# 5 Nightlife and the Arts

# THE ARTS

**T**HE MUSIC AND THEATER SEASON runs from September to June. Information about what's going on in the city can be found in the weekly magazines (published every Wednesday) *Pariscope* (which has an English section), *L'Officiel des Spectacles,* and *Figaroscope* (a supplement to *Le Figaro* newspaper). The Paris Tourist Office (☞ Visitor Information *in* Smart Travel Tips) has a 24-hour hot line in English (☎ 08–36–68–31–12) and a Web site (www.paris-touristoffice.com) listing events.

The best place to buy tickets is at the venue itself; try to purchase in advance, as many of the more popular performances sell out. Also try your hotel or a travel agency, such as **Paris-Vision** (⌧ 1 rue Auber, 9ᵉ, ☎ 01–40–06–01–00, métro Opéra). Tickets for most concerts can be bought at **FNAC** (especially ⌧ 1–5 rue Pierre Lescot, Forum des Halles, 3rd level down, 1ᵉʳ, ☎ 01–49–87–50–50, métro Châtelet–Les Halles). The **Virgin Megastore** (⌧ 52 av. des Champs-Élysées, 8ᵉ, ☎ 08–03–02–30–24, métro Franklin-D.-Roosevelt) also sells theater and concert tickets. Half-price tickets for many same-day theater performances are available at the **Kiosques Théâtre** (⌧ across from 15 Pl. de la Madeleine, métro Madeleine; and ⌧ outside Gare Montparnasse on Pl. Raoul Dautry, 15ᵉ, métro Montparnasse-Bienvenüe); both are open Tuesday–Saturday 12:30–8 and Sunday 12:30–4. Expect to pay a 16-franc commission per ticket and to wait in line.

## Classical Music

Classical- and world-music concerts are held at the **Cité de la Musique** (⌧ 221 av. Jean-Jaurès, 19ᵉ, ☎ 01–44–84–44–84, métro Porte de Pantin). The **Salle Pleyel** (⌧ 252 rue du Faubourg–St-Honoré, 8ᵉ, ☎ 01–45–61–53–00, métro Ternes) is Paris's principal home of classical music. The **Théâtre des Champs-Élysées** (⌧ 15 av. Montaigne, 8ᵉ, ☎ 01–49–52–50–50, métro Alma-Marceau), an Art Deco temple, hosts concerts and ballet. Paris has a never-ending stream of inexpensive lunchtime and evening concerts in churches, some scheduled as part of the **Festival d'Art Sacré** (☎ 01–44–70–64–10 for information) between mid-November and Christmas. **Churches** with classical concerts (often free) include (☞ Chapter 2 *for* addresses): Notre-Dame, Ste-Chapelle, St-Eustache, St-Germain-des-Prés, St-Julien-Le-Pauvre, St-Louis-en-l'Ile, and St-Roch.

## Dance

The **Opéra Garnier** (✉ Pl. de l'Opéra, 9ᵉ, ☎ 08–36–69–78–68, métro Opéra) is home to the reputable Paris Ballet. At the **Théâtre de la Bastille** (✉ 76 rue de la Roquette, 11ᵉ, ☎ 01–43–57–42–14, métro Bastille), innovative modern dance companies perform. The **Théâtre de la Ville** (✉ 2 Pl. du Châtelet, 4ᵉ, ☎ 01–42–74–22–77 for both, métro Châtelet; ✉ 31 rue des Abbesses, 18ᵉ, métro Abbesses) is Paris's temple of contemporary dance.

## Film

Parisians are far more addicted to the cinema as an art form than even Londoners or New Yorkers, as revealed by the number of movie theaters in the city. Many theaters, especially in principal tourist areas such as the Champs-Élysées, St-Germain-des-Prés, Les Halles, and the boulevard des Italiens near the Opéra, show first-run films in English. Check the weekly guides for a movie of your choice. Look for the initials *v.o.,* which mean *version originale,* i.e., not dubbed. Cinema admission runs from 37 to 51 francs; many theaters reduce rates slightly on Monday and for some morning shows. Most theaters will post two show times: The first is the *séance,* when commercials, previews, and sometimes short films start, and the second is the actual feature presentation time, which is usually 10–20 minutes later.

Paris has many small cinemas showing classic and independent films, especially in the Latin Quarter. Screenings are often organized around retrospectives (check "Festivals" in weekly guides). One of the best venues for classic French and international films (Wednesday–Saturday) is the **Cinémathèque Française** (✉ 42 bd. de Bonne-Nouvelle, ☎ 01–

47–04–24–24, métro Bonne-Nouvelle and ⊠ Palais de Chaillot, 7 av. Albert de Mun, ☎ 01–55–73–16–80, métro Trocadéro). The **Max Linder Panorama** (⊠ 24 bd. Poissonnière, 9ᵉ, ☎ 01–48–24–88–88, métro Rue Montmartre) frequently shows classics on its big screen.

## Opera

Getting tickets to the opera can be difficult on short notice, so it's a good idea to plan ahead. For the season's schedule, contact the Opéra de la Bastille (⊠ 120 rue de Lyon, Paris 75012) in advance. Bookings by mail begin roughly two months before the date of performance. Buying from scalpers is not recommended, as they have been known to sell counterfeit tickets. The **Opéra de la Bastille** (⊠ Pl. de la Bastille, 12ᵉ, ☎ 08–36–69–78–68, métro Bastille) has taken over the role as Paris's main opera house from the Opéra Garnier (☞ Dance, *above*).

The **Opéra Comique** (⊠ 5 rue Favart, 2ᵉ, ☎ 01–42–44–45–46, métro Richelieu-Drouot) is a lofty old hall where comic operas are often performed. Better known as the Théâtre du Châtelet, the **Théâtre Musical de Paris** (⊠ Pl. du Châtelet, 1ᵉʳ, ☎ 01–40–28–28–40, métro Châtelet) has built up a strong reputation for opera and other productions.

## Theater

A number of theaters line the Grand Boulevards between Opéra and République, but there is no Paris equivalent to Broadway or the West End. Shows are mostly in French. **Bouffes du Nord** (⊠ 37 bis bd. de la Chapelle, 10ᵉ, ☎ 01–46–07–34–50, métro La Chapelle) is home to English director Peter Brook. The **Comédie-Française** (⊠ Pl. André-Malraux, 1ᵉʳ, ☎ 01–44–58–15–15, métro Palais-Royal) is a distinguished venue that stages classical French drama. The **Théâtre de la Huchette** (⊠ 23 rue de la Huchette, 5ᵉ, ☎ 01–43–26–38–99, métro St-Michel), a tiny Left Bank theater, has been staging Ionesco's *The Bald Soprano* every night since 1950. **Théâtre de l'Odéon** (⊠ Pl. de l'Odéon, 6ᵉ, ☎ 01–44–41–36–36, métro Odéon) has made pan-European theater its primary focus.

# NIGHTLIFE

You've immersed yourself in culture all day and you want
a night out on the town. The hottest spots are around
Ménilmontant, the Bastille, and the Marais. The Left Bank
is definitely a lot less happening. The Champs-Élysées is making a comeback, though the clientele remains predominantly foreign. Take note: The last métro runs between 12:30
AM and 1 AM (you can take a taxi, but they can be hard to
find, especially on weekend nights).

## Bars and Clubs

It helps to be famous—or look like a model—to get into
**Les Bains** (⊠ 7 rue du Bourg-l'Abbé, 3ᵉ, ☏ 01–48–87–01–
80, métro Étienne-Marcel), a forever-trendy club (closed
Monday). **Le Cabaret** (⊠ 68 rue de Charonne, 8ᵉ, ☏ 01–
42–89–44–14, métro Franklin-D.-Roosevelt) used to be
just that; now there are still cabaret acts, as well as danc-
ing to soul and funk. **Café Charbon** (⊠ 109 rue Oberkampf,
11ᵉ, ☏ 01–43–57–55–13, métro St-Maur, Parmentier) is a
beautifully restored 19th-century café with a trendsetting
crowd. **Le Comptoir** (⊠ 5 rue Monsieur-Le-Prince, 6ᵉ, ☏
01–43–29–12–05, Odéon) is a traditional wine bar serving Burgundy and Bordeaux by the glass. **L'Élysée Montmartre** (⊠ 72 bd. de Rochechouart, 18ᵉ, ☏ 01–44–92–45–
45, métro Anvers) hosts the hottest club nights in Paris on
Saturday (during the week it's a concert hall). **Le Fumoir**
(⊠ 6 rue Amiral de Coligny, 1ᵉʳ, ☏ 01–42–92–00–24,
métro Louvre), a fashionable spot for cocktails, has a large
bar, library, and comfy leather couches. **Man Ray** (⊠ 34
rue Marbeuf, 8ᵉ, ☏ 01–56–88–36–36, métro Franklin-D.-
Roosevelt), owned by Sean Penn, Johnny Depp, and Mick
Hucknall, has a spacious mezzanine bar overlooking an
Asian-inspired dining room. **Le What's Up Bar** (⊠ 15 rue
Daval, 11ᵉ, ☏ 01–48–05–88–33, métro Bastille) is a hip,
modern spot where trendy DJs play house and garage
music after 10:30 PM; on weekends there's a 50-franc cover.

### Gay and Lesbian Bars and Clubs

Gay and lesbian bars and clubs are mostly concentrated in
the Marais and include some of the most happening addresses in the city. **Le Dépôt** (⊠ 10 rue aux Ours, 3ᵉ, ☏ 01–

44–54–96–96, métro Etienne Marcel) is a bar, club, and back room for men. The mostly male crowd at **L'Open Café** (⊠ 17 rue des Archives, 4ᵉ, ☎ 01–42–72–26–18, métro Hôtel-de-Ville) comes for the sunny decor and convivial ambience. **Le Pulp!** (⊠ 25 bd. Poissonnière, 2ᵉ, ☎ 01–40–26–01–93, métro Grands Boulevards) is one of the few lesbian-only nightclubs in Paris. **Queen** (⊠ 102 av. des Champs-Élysées, 8ᵉ, ☎ 01–53–89–08–90, métro George-V) is one of the hottest nightspots in Paris: Although it's predominantly gay, everyone else lines up to get in, too.

### Hotel Bars

Paris's hotel bars are highly popular nostalgic spots as well as quiet, elegant places to talk. **Bristol** (⊠ 112 rue du Faubourg–St-Honoré, 8ᵉ, ☎ 01–53–43–43–42, métro Miromesnil). **Lutétia** (⊠ 45 bd. Raspail, 6ᵉ, ☎ 01–49–54–46–09, métro Sèvres-Babylone). **Ritz Hemingway Bar** (⊠ 15 Pl. Vendôme, 1ᵉʳ, ☎ 01–43–16–33–65, métro Opéra).

# Cabaret

Paris's cabarets are household names, though mostly tourists go to them these days. Prices range from 200 francs (simple admission plus one drink) to more than 800 francs (dinner plus show). **Crazy Horse** (⊠ 12 av. George-V, 8ᵉ, ☎ 01–47–23–32–32, métro Alma-Marceau) is one of the best-known cabarets, with pretty dancers and raunchy routines. **Lido** (⊠ 116 bis av. des Champs-Élysées, 8ᵉ, ☎ 01–40–76–56–10, métro George-V) stars the famous Bluebell Girls; the owners claim that no show in Las Vegas can rival it for special effects. That old favorite at the foot of Montmartre, **Moulin Rouge** (⊠ Pl. Blanche, 18ᵉ, ☎ 01–53–09–82–82, métro Blanche), mingles the Doriss Girls, the cancan, and a horse in an extravagant spectacle. **Paradis Latin** (⊠ 28 rue du Cardinal Lemoine, 5ᵉ, ☎ 01–43–25–28–28, métro Cardinal Lemoine) is the liveliest and trendiest cabaret on the Left Bank.

# Jazz Clubs

Paris is one of the great jazz cities of the world. For nightly schedules consult the specialty magazines *Jazz Hot* or *Jazz Magazine*. Nothing gets going till 10 PM or 11 PM; entry

prices vary widely from about 40 francs to more than 100
francs. At the Méridien Hotel, near Porte Maillot, the **Lionel Hampton Jazz Club** (⊠ 81 bd. Gouvion-St-Cyr, 17ᵉ,
☎ 01–40–68–30–42, métro Porte Maillot) hosts a roster
of international jazz players. **New Morning** (⊠ 7 rue des
Petites-Écuries, 10ᵉ, ☎ 01–45–23–51–41, métro Château-
d'Eau) is a premier spot for serious fans of avant-garde jazz,
as well as folk and world music. The greatest names in French
and international jazz have been playing at **Le Petit Journal** (⊠ 71 bd. St-Michel, 5ᵉ, ☎ 01–43–26–28–59, RER Luxembourg) for decades; it now specializes in Dixieland jazz
(it's closed Sunday). **Le Petit Opportun** (⊠ 15 rue des La-
vandières-Ste-Opportune, 1ᵉʳ, ☎ 01–42–36–01–36, métro
Châtelet), in a converted bistro, often features top-flight
American soloists with French backup.

## Rock, Pop, and World Music Venues

Upcoming concerts are posted on boards in FNAC and Virgin Megastores. **Le Bataclan** (⊠ 50 bd. Voltaire, 11ᵉ, ☎ 01–
48–06–28–12, métro Oberkampf) is an intimate venue for
live rock, rap, and reggae. **L'Élysée Montmartre** (☞ Bars
and Clubs, *above*) is one of the prime venues for emerging
French and international rock groups. **L'Olympia** (⊠ 28 bd.
des Capucines, 9ᵉ, ☎ 01–47–42–25–49, métro Madeleine),
a legendary venue once favored by Jacques Brel and Edith
Piaf, still plays host to leading French vocalists. **Zenith** (⊠
Parc de la Villette, 19ᵉ, ☎ 01–42–08–60–00, métro Porte-
de-Pantin) stages large rock shows.

# 6 Outdoor Activities and Sports

# Participant Sports

## Bicycling

Paris has been making valiant efforts to become more bi-
cycle-friendly. More than 125 km (78 mi) of bicycle lanes
now cross the city, notably along rue de Rivoli and boulevard St-Germain. Certain roads are banned to cars altogether
on Sunday (including the banks of the Seine along quai de
la Tournelle from 9 to 6 and the roads alongside the Canal
St-Martin from 2 to 6). Paris's two large parks, the Bois
de Boulogne (☞ Chapter 2) and the Bois de Vincennes (métro
Porte Dorée, Château de Vincennes) are also good places
for biking. Bikes can be rented from the following: **Maison
Roue Libre** (⊠ 95 bis rue Rambuteau, 4ᵉ, ☎ 01–40–28–00–
77, métro Rambuteau, Châtelet–Les Halles); **Pariscyclo**
(⊠ Rond Point de Jardin d'Acclimatation, in the Bois de
Boulogne, 16ᵉ, ☎ 01–47–47–76–50, métro Les Sablons);
and **Paris à Vélo, C'est Sympa** (⊠ 37 bd. Bourdon, 4ᵉ, ☎
01–48–87–60–01, métro Bastille).

## Health Clubs and Swimming Pools

A number of hotels, gyms, and clubs in the city offer one-
day or short-term memberships. **Aquaboulevard de Paris**
(⊠ 4 rue Louis-Armand, 15ᵉ, ☎ 01–40–60–10–00, métro
Balard) has a gym, Turkish baths, and the city's best swimming pool, complete with giant slide and wave machine (150
francs per day). **Club Quartier Latin** (⊠ 19 rue de Pontoise,
5ᵉ, ☎ 01–55–42–77–88, métro Maubert Mutualité) has a
30-meter skylighted pool, a climbing wall, squash courts,
and exercise equipment (70 francs per day and 75 francs
per 40 minutes of squash). **Espace Vit'Halles** (⊠ 48 rue Rambuteau, 3ᵉ, ☎ 01–42–77–21–71, métro Rambuteau) has a
broad range of aerobics classes (100 francs a class), exercise machines, a sauna, and a steam bath. The **Piscine des
Halles** (⊠ entrance on Pl. de la Rotonde, in the Forum des
Halles, 1ᵉʳ, ☎ 01–42–36–98–44) is a 50-meter public pool;
admission is 25 francs; call for hours.

## Jogging

The best place to run in the city is in the **Champ de Mars,**
next to the Eiffel Tower, measuring 2 km (1¼ mi) around
the perimeter. Shorter and more crowded routes are found
in the **Jardin du Luxembourg,** with a 1½-km (about 1-mi)
loop just inside the park's fence. The path in the **Jardin des**

**Tuileries** also measures about 1½ km (1 mi). The **Parc Monceau** has a loop of 1 km (about ½ mi). The **Bois de Boulogne** (☞ Chapter 2) has miles of trails through woods and around lakes. The equally bucolic **Bois de Vincennes** has a 15-km (9⅓-mi) circuit or a 1½-km (1-mi) loop around the Château de Vincennes itself.

## Rollerblading

A popular site for rollerblading is along the Promenade Plantée, running along the former viaduct in the 12ᵉ arrondissement, as well as along the Seine and the Canal St-Martin (☞ Bicycling, *above*). Every Friday night starting at 10, hundreds of people gather at Place de l'Italie to rollerblade together through Paris (roads are blocked off); for details, check their Web site (www.pari-roller.com). Rollerblades can be rented from **Bike 'n Roller** (⊠ 6 rue St-Julien le Pauvre, 5ᵉ, ☎ 01–44–07–35–89) for 25 francs an hour and 75 francs per day. **Roller Location Nomades** (⊠ 37 bd. Bourdon, 4ᵉ, ☎ 01–44–54–07–44) rents skates for 50–60 francs per day.

# Spectator Sports

Information on upcoming events can be found in the weekly guide *Pariscope,* on posters around the city, or by calling the ticket agency of **FNAC** (☎ 01–49–87–50–50). A wide range of sporting events takes place at the **Palais Omnisports de Paris-Bercy** (⊠ 8 bd. de Bercy, 12ᵉ, ☎ 01–44–68–44–68, métro Bercy). The **Parc des Princes** (⊠ 24 rue du Cdt. Guilbaud, 16ᵉ, ☎ 01–42–88–02–76, métro Porte de St-Cloud) is where the city's soccer team, Paris St-Germain, plays its home matches. **Roland-Garros** (⊠ 2 av. Gordon Bennett, 16ᵉ, ☎ 01–47–43–48–00, métro Porte d'Auteuil) is the venue for the French Open tennis tournament in May. **Stade de France** (⊠ St-Denis, ☎ 01–55–93–00–00, RER La Plaine–Stade de France) was built for the World Cup in 1998 and is now home to the French national soccer and rugby teams.

# 7  Shopping

**T**HE SHOPPING OPPORTUNITIES in Paris are endless and geared to every taste. Perfume and designer clothing are perhaps the most coveted Parisian souvenirs. Yet you'll pay the going rate for them because even on haute couture's home turf, bargains are surprisingly elusive. It's good to be aware of the slings and arrows of international exchange rates and to know prices at home before you arrive.

Revised
and
updated by
Ian Phillips

When hunting for bargains, watch for the word *soldes* (sales): The two main sale seasons are January and July. For nice gifts try the shops in Paris's museums, especially the Louvre, the Musée Carnavalet, the Opéra Garnier, and the Musée des Arts Décoratifs.

If you're from outside the European Union, age 15 and over, and stay in France and/or the European Union for less than six months, you can benefit from Value Added Tax (VAT) reimbursements, known in France as TVA or *détaxe*. To qualify, non-EU residents must spend at least 2,000 francs in a single store. Refunds vary from 13% to 20.6% and are mailed to you by check or credited to your charge card. For more information on VAT refunds, *see* Taxes *in* Smart Travel Tips.

## Shopping by Neighborhood

### Avenue Montaigne

This exclusive, elegant boulevard and the area around it are a showcase of international haute-couture houses: **Chanel, Dior, Nina Ricci, Jil Sander, Jean-Louis Scherrer, Emanuel Ungaro, Céline, Valentino, MaxMara, Genny, Krizia, Escada, Thierry Mugler, Hanae Mori, Calvin Klein, Prada,** and **Dolce & Gabbana.** You'll also find accessories by **S. T. Dupont, Loewe, Salvatore Ferragamo,** and **Louis Vuitton.** Neighboring rue François 1er and avenue George V are also lined with many designer boutiques: **Versace, Yves St-Laurent, Balenciaga,** and **Givenchy.**

### Champs-Élysées

Cafés and movie theaters keep the once-chic Champs-Élysées active 24 hours a day, but the invasion of exchange banks, car showrooms, and fast-food chains has lowered the tone. Four glitzy 20th-century arcade malls—**Galerie du Lido, Le Rond-Point, Le Claridge,** and **Élysées 26**—capture most of the retail action, not to mention the **Gap** and the **Disney Store.** The opening of the new Peter Marino–designed **Louis Vuitton** boutique and the cosmetic wonder store **Sephora** have reintroduced a touch of elegance.

## The Faubourg St-Honoré

This chic shopping and residential street is exemplified by the presence of the Élysée Palace and the official residences of the American and British ambassadors. The Paris branches of **Sotheby's** and **Christie's** and renowned antiques galleries such as **Didier Aaron** add artistic flavor. Boutiques include **Hermès, Lanvin, Gucci, Chloé, Guy Laroche,** and **Christian Lacroix.**

## Left Bank

After decades of clustering on the Right Bank's venerable shopping avenues, the high-fashion houses have stormed the Rive Gauche. The first to arrive were **Sonia Rykiel** and **Yves St-Laurent** in the late '60s. Some of the more recent arrivals include **Christian Dior, Giorgio Armani,** and **Louis Vuitton.** Rue des St-Pères and rue de Grenelle are lined with designer names; the latter is especially known for its top-quality shoe shops, such as **Christian Louboutin, Sergio Rossi, Patrick Cox, Stéphane Kélian,** and Michel Perry's less expensive line, **Stephen.**

## Les Halles

Most of the narrow pedestrian streets on the former site of Paris's wholesale food market are lined with fast-food joints, sex shops, jeans outlets, and souvenir stands. But rue du Jour, featuring **Agnès B., Diapositive,** and **Zadig & Voltaire,** is an attractive exception. Not far away, rue Tiquetonne is a mecca for retro cool. In the middle of the action is the **Forum des Halles,** a multilevel underground shopping mall, which, though it has its share of teens and chain stores, also has begun attracting higher-quality merchants and a clutch of promising designers.

## Louvre–Palais Royal

The elegant and eclectic shops clustered in the 18th-century arcades of the Palais-Royal sell such items as an-

# Finally, a travel companion that doesn't snore on the plane or eat all your peanuts.

When traveling, your MCI WorldCom Card is the best way to keep in touch. Our operators speak your language, so they'll be able to connect you back home—no matter where your travels take you. Plus, your MCI WorldCom Card is easy to use, and even earns you frequent flyer miles every time you use it. When you add in our great rates, you get something even more valuable: peace-of-mind. So go ahead. Travel the world. MCI WorldCom just brought it a whole lot closer.

You can even sign up today at www.mci.com/worldphone or ask your operator to make a collect call to 1-410-314-2938.

## EASY TO CALL WORLDWIDE

1 Just dial the WorldPhone access number of the country you're calling from.
2 Dial or give the operator your MCI WorldCom Card number.
3 Dial or give the number you're calling.

| Argentina | |
|---|---|
| To call using Telefonica | 0-800-222-6249 |
| To call using Telecom | 0-800-555-1002 |
| **Brazil** | 000-8012 |
| **France ◆** | 0-800-99-0019 |
| **Ireland** | 1-800-55-1001 |
| **United Kingdom** | |
| To call using BT | 0800-89-0222 |
| To call using CWC | 0500-89-0222 |
| **United States** | 1-800-888-8000 |

For your complete WorldPhone calling guide, dial the WorldPhone access number for the country you're in and ask the operator for Customer Service. In the U.S. call 1-800-431-5402.

◆ Public phones may require deposit of coin or phone card for dial tone.

## EARN FREQUENT FLYER MILES

MCI WorldCom, its logo and the names of the products referred to herein are proprietary marks of MCI WorldCom, Inc. All airline names and logos are proprietary marks of the respective airlines. All airline program rules and conditions apply.

# The first thing you need overseas is the one thing you forget to pack.

---

## FOREIGN CURRENCY DELIVERED OVERNIGHT

---

Chase Currency To Go® delivers foreign currency to your home
by the next business day*

It's easy—before you travel, call
1-888-CHASE84 for delivery of any
of 75 currencies

Delivery is free with orders of
$500 or more

Competitive rates—
without exchange fees

You don't have to be a Chase
customer—you can pay by Visa®
or MasterCard®

---

**◻ CHASE**

THE RIGHT RELATIONSHIP IS EVERYTHING.®

**1•888•CHASE84**
www.chase.com

tiques, toy soldiers, cosmetics, jewelry, and vintage designer dresses. The glossy, marble **Carrousel du Louvre** mall, beneath the Louvre Museum, is lighted by an immense inverted glass pyramid. Shops, including a **Virgin Megastore, The Body Shop,** and **Esprit,** along with a lively international food court, are open on Sunday—still a rare convenience in Paris.

## Le Marais

Between the pre-Revolution mansions and tiny kosher food shops that characterize this area are scores of trendy gift and clothing stores. Avant-garde designers **Azzedine Alaïa, Lolita Lempicka, Issey Miyake,** and **Atsuro Tayamap** have boutiques within a few blocks of the stately Place des Vosges and the Picasso and Carnavalet museums. The Marais is one of the few neighborhoods where shops are open on Sunday.

## Opéra to La Madeleine

Three major department stores—**Au Printemps, Galeries Lafayette,** and the British **Marks & Spencer**—define boulevard Haussmann, behind Paris's ornate 19th-century Opéra Garnier. Place de la Madeleine is home to two luxurious food stores, **Fauchon** and **Hédiard.** Steps away, on boulevard de la Madeleine, is a classy 75-shop mall, **Les Trois Quartiers. Lalique** and **Baccarat** crystal also have opulent showrooms near the Église de la Madeleine.

## Passy–Victor Hugo

The residential and staid 16ᵉ arrondissement attracts predictably classic and upscale retailers, most of whom are centered on **rue de Passy**—such as **Franck et Fils**—and **Place Victor Hugo.** At a handful of secondhand shops in this wealthy area, exceptionally good deals can be found. **Réciproque,** on rue de la Pompe, for instance, is one of the biggest and best discount haunts in Paris.

## Place Vendôme and Rue de la Paix

The magnificent 17th-century Place Vendôme, home of the Ritz Hotel, and rue de la Paix, leading north from Vendôme, are where you can find the world's most elegant jewelers: **Cartier, Boucheron, Buccellati, Van Cleef and Arpels, Répossi, Mauboussin,** and **Mikimoto.** The most exclusive, however, is the discreet **Jar's.**

## Place des Victoires and Rue Etienne Marcel

The graceful, circular Place des Victoires, near the Palais-Royal, is the playground of cutting-edge fashion icons such as **Kenzo, Victoire,** and **Thierry Mugler.** Seriously avant-garde designers like **Comme des Garçons, Yohji Yamamoto,** and **Marithé & François Girbaud** line rue Etienne Marcel. In the nearby **Galerie Vivienne** shopping arcade, **Jean-Paul Gaultier** has a shop. And at No. 3 rue d'Argout, one of the hottest clubwear emporiums in the neighborhood, **Le Shop,** rents retail space to hip, up-and-coming designers.

## Rue St-Honoré

A fashionable set makes its way to rue St-Honoré to shop at Paris's most trendy boutique, **Colette.** The street is lined with numerous designer names, as well as the delightful vintage jewelry store **Dary's.** On nearby rue Cambon, you'll find the wonderfully elegant **Maria Luisa** and the main **Chanel** boutique.

# Department Stores

Paris's top department stores offer both convenience and style. Most are open Monday through Saturday from about 9:30 AM to 7 PM, and some are open until 10 PM one weekday evening. All six major stores listed below have multilingual guides, international welcome desks, détaxe offices, and restaurants. Most are on the Right Bank, near the Opéra and the Hôtel de Ville; the notable exception is Au Bon Marché on the Left Bank.

**Au Bon Marché** (⌧ 24 rue de Sèvres, 7ᵉ, ☎ 01–44–39–80–00, métro Sèvres-Babylone), founded in 1852, is an excellent hunting ground on the Left Bank for linens, table settings, and high-quality furniture. The ground-floor Balthazar men's shop feels like a smart boutique. La Grande Épicerie (☞ Food and Wine *in* Specialty Shops, *below*) is one of the largest groceries in Paris and a gourmet's mecca, and the basement is a treasure trove for books, records, classy stationery, and artsy gifts.

**Au Printemps** (⌧ 64 bd. Haussmann, 9ᵉ, ☎ 01–42–82–50–00, métro Havre-Caumartin, Opéra, or Auber) has three floors of women's fashion featuring designers like Helmut

Lang, Dolce & Gabbana, and Zara. Free fashion shows are held on Tuesday (all year) and Friday (Apr.–Oct.) at 10 AM under the cupola on the seventh floor of La Mode, the building dedicated to women's and children's fashion. (Reservations can be made in advance by calling ☎ 01–42–82–63–17; tickets can also be obtained on the day of show at the service desk on the first floor.) The three-store complex also includes La Maison, for housewares and furniture, and Brummel, a six-floor emporium devoted to menswear. Flo Prestige, the celebrated Parisian brasserie chain, runs the in-house restaurant.

**Bazar de l'Hôtel de Ville** (✉ 52–64 rue de Rivoli, 4ᵉ, ☎ 01–42–74–90–00, métro Hôtel de Ville), better known as BHV, houses an enormous basement hardware store that sells everything from doorknobs to cement mixers. The fashion offerings are minimal, but BHV is noteworthy for quality household goods, home decor materials, and office supplies.

**Galeries Lafayette** (✉ 40 bd. Haussmann, 9ᵉ, ☎ 01–42–82–34–56, métro Chaussée d'Antin, Opéra, or Havre-Caumartin; ✉ Centre Commercial Montparnasse, 15ᵉ, ☎ 01–45–38–52–87, métro Montparnasse-Bienvenüe) carries nearly 80,000 fashion labels under its roof. Free fashion shows are held every Wednesday at 11 AM (☎ 01–48–74–02–30 for reservations). Along with the world's largest perfumery, the main store has the "Espace Lafayette Maison," a huge Yves Taralon–designed emporium dedicated to the art of living *à la française*. There's also a gourmet food hall, a separate men's store, and a sports shop.

**Marks & Spencer** (✉ 35 bd. Haussmann, 9ᵉ, ☎ 01–47–42–42–91, métro Havre-Caumartin, Auber, or Opéra; ✉ 88 rue de Rivoli, 4ᵉ, ☎ 01–44–61–08–00, métro Hôtel de Ville) is a British chain chiefly noted for its moderately priced basics (underwear, socks, sleep- and sportswear) as well as its popular English grocery store and take-out.

**La Samaritaine** (✉ 19 rue de la Monnaie, 1ᵉʳ, ☎ 01–40–41–20–20, métro Pont-Neuf or Châtelet), a sprawling five-store complex, carries everything from designer fashions to cuckoo clocks but is especially known for kitchen supplies, housewares, and furniture. Its most famous asset is the Toupary restaurant in Building 2, from which there's a marvelous view of Notre-Dame and the Left Bank.

106

À la Mère de Famille, **20**

L'Absinthe, **33**

L'Artisan Parfumeur, **39**

Au Bon Marché, **53**

Au Nain Bleu, **10**

Au Printemps, **16**

Bazar de l'Hôtel de Ville, **42**

Berluti, **4**

Brentano's, **26**

By Terry, **37**

Le Cave Augé, **11**

Chacok, **46**

Chanel, **2, 13**

Charvet, **25**

Christian Dior, **3**

Christian Laboutin, **36**

Christian Liaigre, **44**

Colette, **30**

Compagnie Français, **48**

Dary's, **23**

Dipaki, **15**

Diptyque, **50**

Du Pareil Au Même, **17**

L'Epicerie, **38**

Et Vous, **9**

Façonnable, **8**

Galeries Lafayette, **19, 54**

Galerie Vivienne, **28**

Jean-Paul Gaultier, **27**

La Maison du Chocolat, **5, 7, 14**

Maria Luisa, **24**

Marks & Spencer, **18, 40**

Michel Perry, **32**

Panoplie, **35**

Passage des Panoramas, **22**

Passage des Pavillons, **29**

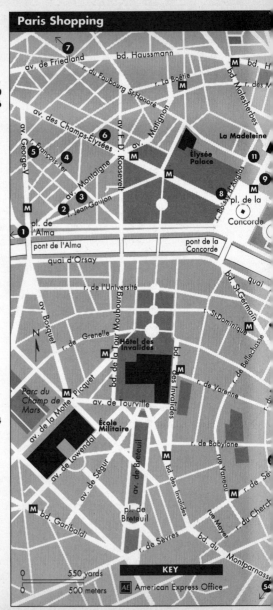

**Paris Shopping**

Passage
Jouffroy, **21**
Réciproque, **1**
Sabbia Rosa, **47**
La
Samaritaine, **41**
Sentou Galerie, **43**
Shakespeare &
Company, **51**
Shoe Bizz, **45**
Stéphane
Kélian, **12, 34**
Tara Jarmon, **49**
Victoire, **31**
Village Voice, **52**
Zara, **6**

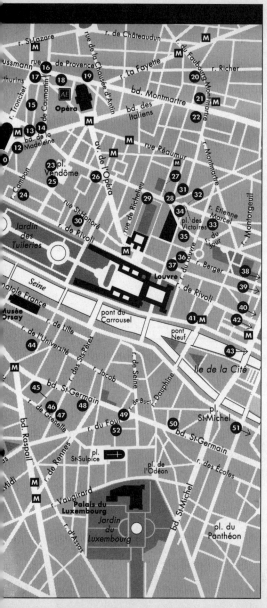

## Budget

**Monoprix** and **Prisunic** are French dime stores—with scores of branches throughout the city—that stock inexpensive everyday items like toothpaste, groceries, toys, and paper—a little of everything. Both chains carry inexpensive children's clothes and makeup of surprisingly good quality.

# Markets

## Flea Markets

**Le Marché aux Puces St-Ouen** (métro Porte de Clignancourt), on Paris's northern boundary, still attracts the crowds when it opens on weekends and Monday, but its once-unbeatable prices are now a feature of the past. This century-old labyrinth of alleyways packed with antiques dealers' booths and junk stalls spreads for over a square mile. Arrive early to pick up the most worthwhile loot (like old prints). But be warned—if there's one place in Paris where you need to know how to bargain, this is it! For lunch, stop for mussels and fries in one of the rough-and-ready cafés.

On the southern and eastern slopes of the city—at **Porte de Montreuil** and **Porte de Vanves**—are other, less-impressive flea markets. Both have an enormous amount of junk to sift through to find any real bargains.

## Food Markets

Paris's open-air food markets are among the city's most colorful attractions. Fruits and vegetables are piled high in vibrant pyramids. The variety of cheeses is always astounding. The lively—and somewhat chaotic—atmosphere that reigns in most markets makes them a sight worth seeing, even if you don't want or need to buy anything. Every *quartier* (neighborhood) has at least one, although many are open only a few days each week. Sunday morning, till 1 PM, is usually a good time to go; Monday they are likely to be closed.

Many of the better-known markets are in areas you'd visit for sightseeing: **rue de Buci** (⊠ 6ᵉ, métro Odéon, ☉ daily) near St-Germain-des-Prés; **rue Mouffetard** (⊠ 5ᵉ, métro Monge, best on weekends) near the Jardin des Plantes; **rue Montorgueil** (⊠ 1ᵉʳ, métro Châtelet–Les Halles, ☉ daily);

**rue Lepic** in Montmartre (⊠ 18ᵉ, métro Blanche or Abbesses, best on weekends); **rue Lévis** (⊠ 17ᵉ, métro Villiers, ☉ daily) near Parc Monceau.

# Shopping Arcades

Paris's 19th-century commercial arcades, called *passages* or *galeries* are the forerunners of the modern mall. Glass roofs, decorative pillars, and mosaic floors give the passages character. The major arcades are on the Right Bank in central Paris. **Galerie Vivienne** (⊠ 4 rue des Petits-Champs, 2ᵉ, métro Bourse) is home to a range of interesting shops, an excellent tearoom, and a quality wine shop. **Passage Jouffroy** (⊠ 12 bd. Montmartre, 2ᵉ, métro Montmartre) is full of shops selling toys, postcards, antique canes, and perfumes. **Passage des Panoramas** (⊠ 11 bd. Montmartre, 2ᵉ, métro Montmartre), built in 1800, is the oldest of them all. The elegant **Passage des Pavillons** (⊠ 6 rue de Beaujolais, 1ᵉʳ, métro Palais-Royal) has shops selling gourmet foods and antiquarian books.

# Specialty Stores

## Accessories, Cosmetics, and Perfumes

**L'Artisan Parfumeur** (⊠ 32 rue du Bourg Tibourg, 4ᵉ, ☎ 01–48–04–55–66, métro Hôtel de Ville) sells its own brand of scents. **By Terry** (⊠ 21 Galerie Véro Dodat, 1ᵉʳ, ☎ 01–44–76–00–76, métro Louvre), the brainchild of Yves St-Laurent's director of makeup, Terry de Gunzberg, carries "ready-to-wear" makeup as well as personalized cosmetics. **Christian Louboutin** (⊠ 19 rue Jean-Jacques Rousseau, 1ᵉʳ, ☎ 01–42–36–05–31, métro Louvre) is famous for his wacky but elegant shoes, trademark blood-red soles, and impressive client list (Caroline of Monaco, Catherine Deneuve, Liz Taylor). **Dary's** (⊠ 362 rue St-Honoré, 1ᵉʳ, ☎ 01–42–60–95–23, métro Tuileries) is a treasure trove of antique jewelry, favored by models and fashion stylists. **Michel Perry** (⊠ 4 rue des Petits Pères, 2ᵉ, ☎ 01–42–44–10–04, métro Palais-Royal) is famous for his elegant, slender high-heel shoes. **Sabbia Rosa** (⊠ 73 rue des Saints-Pères, 6ᵉ, ☎ 01–45–48–88–37, métro St-Germain-des-Prés) sells French lingerie.

## Antiques

Antiques dealers proliferate in the **Carré Rive Gauche** (⊠ between St-Germain-des-Prés and the Musée d'Orsay, 6ᵉ, métro St-Germain-des-Prés, Rue du Bac).

## Bookstores (English-Language)

The scenic open-air bookstalls along the Seine sell secondhand books (mostly in French), prints, and souvenirs. Numerous French-language bookstores—specializing in a wide range of topics, including art, film, literature, and philosophy—are found in the Latin Quarter and around St-Germain-des-Prés. For English-language books try these stores. **Brentano's** (⊠ 37 av. de l'Opéra, 2ᵉ, ☎ 01–42–61–52–50, métro Opéra) is stocked with everything from classics to children's titles. **Shakespeare & Co.** (⊠ 37 rue de la Bûcherie, 5ᵉ, ☎ 01–43–26–96–50, métro St-Michel) specializes in expatriate literature. **Village Voice** (⊠ 6 rue Princesse, 6ᵉ, ☎ 01–46–33–36–47, métro Mabillon) hosts regular literary readings.

## Clothing

### CHILDRENSWEAR

**Dipaki** (⊠ 18 rue Vignon, 8ᵉ, ☎ 01–42–66–24–74, métro Madeleine) is a mecca for affordably priced infants' and kids' clothing in bold, primary colors. **Du Pareil Au Même** (⊠ 15 and 23 rue des Mathurins, 8ᵉ, ☎ 01–42–66–93–80, métro Havre-Caumartin; ⊠ 14 rue St-Placide, 6ᵉ, ☎ 01–40–49–00–33, métro St-Placide) is a moderately priced chain selling adorable well-made basics in soft, brightly colored jerseys and cottons.

### MENSWEAR

**Berluti** (⊠ 26 rue Marbeuf, 8ᵉ, ☎ 01–53–93–97–97, métro Franklin-D.-Roosevelt) has been making the most exclusive shoes for men for more than a century. **Charvet** (⊠ 28 Pl. Vendôme, 1ᵉʳ, ☎ 01–42–60–30–70, métro Opéra) is the Parisian equivalent of a Savile Row tailor. **Façonnable** (⊠ 9 rue du Faubourg–St-Honoré, 8ᵉ, ☎ 01–47–42–72–60, métro Concorde) sells fashionable town and weekend clothes for young urbanites. **Panoplie** (⊠ 41 rue Coquillière, 1ᵉʳ, ☎ 01–40–28–90–35, métro Les Halles) is one of the best addresses in town for men's designer fashions.

WOMENSWEAR

**L'Absinthe** (⊠ 74–76 rue Jean-Jacques Rousseau, 1ᵉʳ, ☎ 01–42–33–54–44, métro Les Halles) is a magical address with clothing that's new but looks vintage. **Chacok** (⊠ 18 rue de Grenelle, 6ᵉ, ☎ 01–42–22–69–99, métro Sèvres-Babylone) is *the* label for fashion-savvy Parisians, who adore its colorful, feminine collections. **Chanel** (⊠ 42 av. Montaigne, 8ᵉ, ☎ 01–47–23–74–12, métro Franklin-D.-Roosevelt; ⊠ 31 rue Cambon, 1ᵉʳ, ☎ 01–42–86–28–00, métro Tuileries) is helmed by Karl Lagerfeld, a master at updating Coco's signature look with fresh colors and free-spirited silhouettes. **Christian Dior** (⊠ 30 av. Montaigne, 8ᵉ, ☎ 01–40–73–56–07, métro Franklin-D.-Roosevelt) installed flamboyant British designer John Galliano as head designer after his triumphant run at Givenchy. His dramatic creations, however, have little to do with the Dior tradition. **Colette** (⊠ 213 rue St-Honoré, 1ᵉ, ☎ 01–55–35–33–90, métro Tuileries) is an enormous minimalist space showcasing all that's trendy in fashion, home design, art, and accessories. **Jean-Paul Gaultier** (⊠ 6 rue Vivienne, 2ᵉ, ☎ 01–42–86–05–05, métro Bourse or Palais-Royal), who made his name as Madonna's irreverent clothier, continues to create outrageously attention-getting garments for men and women. **L'Epicerie** (⊠ 30 rue du Temple, 4ᵉ, ☎ 01–42–78–12–39, métro Hôtel de Ville), a cross between a boutique and an art gallery, carries the collections of young, international designers. **Et Vous** (⊠ 25 rue Royale, 8ᵉ, ☎ 01–47–42–31–00, métro Madeleine) is where hip Parisiennes find stylish, contemporary women's wear. **Maria Luisa** (⊠ 2 rue Cambon, 1ᵉʳ, ☎ 01–47–03–96–15, métro Concorde) stocks designers such as Martin Margiela, Jean-Paul Gaultier, and Ann Demeulemeester. **Réciproque** (⊠ 88, 89, 92, 95, 101, and 123 rue de la Pompe, 16ᵉ, ☎ 01–47–04–30–28, métro Rue de la Pompe) is Paris's largest and most exclusive swap shop; savings on designer wear—Hermès, Dior, Chanel—are significant. **Tara Jarmon** (⊠ 18 rue du Four, 6ᵉ, ☎ 01–46–33–26–60, métro Mabillon) is a Canadian designer who has garnered plaudits from Paris's trendwatchers. Her understated, classic knee-length coats are especially popular. **Victoire** (⊠ 10 and 12 Pl. des Victoires, 2ᵉ, ☎ 01–42–61–09–02, métro Bourse or Palais-Royal; menswear at ⊠ 10–12 rue du Colonel Driant, 1ᵉʳ, ☎ 01–42–97–44–87, métro Palais-Royal) stocks a range of

designer labels under one roof, such as Donna Karan,
Lawrence Steele, Narciso Rodriguez, and Alessandro del-
l'Acqua; next door is Victoire's own label. The men's store
is just a stone's throw away on rue du Colonel Driant. **Zara**
(⊠ 44 av. des Champs-Élysées, 8ᵉ, ☎ 01–45–61–52–80,
métro Franklin-D.-Roosevelt) is where smart Parisians pick
up the latest trends at bargain prices.

## Food and Wine

**À la Mère de Famille** (⊠ 35 rue du Faubourg-Montmartre,
9ᵉ, ☎ 01–47–70–83–69, métro Cadet) is well versed in
French regional specialties and old-fashioned bonbons,
sugar candy, and more. **Le Cave Augé** (⊠ 116 bd. Haussmann, 8ᵉ, ☎ 01–45–22–16–97, métro St-Augustin) has
been one of the best wine shops in Paris since 1850. **La Maison du Chocolat** (⊠ 56 rue Pierre-Charron, 8ᵉ, ☎ 01–47–
23–38–25, métro Franklin-D.-Roosevelt; ⊠ 8 bd. de la
Madeleine, 9ᵉ, ☎ 01–47–42–86–52, métro Madeleine; ⊠
225 rue du Faubourg–St-Honoré, 8ᵉ, ☎ 01–42–27–39–44,
métro Ternes) is the place for chocolate; take home some
or go to the tearoom at rue Pierre Charron or Madeleine.

## Housewares and Gifts

**Christian Liaigre** (⊠ 42 rue du Bac, 7ᵉ, ☎ 01–53–63–33–
66, métro Rue du Bac) is one of the world's most fashionable interior decorators; his chicly simple furniture is sold
in his flagship boutique. **Compagnie Française de l'Orient
et de la Chine** (⊠ 163 bd. St-Germain, 6ᵉ, ☎ 01–45–48–
00–18, métro St-Germain-des-Prés) imports beautiful ceramics and furniture from China and Mongolia. **Diptyque**
(⊠ 34 bd. St-Germain, 5ᵉ, ☎ 01–43–26–45–27, métro
Maubert-Mutualité) sells the best scented candles in Paris.
**Sentou Galerie** (⊠ 24 rue du Pont Louis-Philippe, 4ᵉ, ☎ 01–
42–71–00–01, métro St-Paul) has lights designed by artists,
furniture made by young designers, and funky tableware.

## Shoes

**Shoe Bizz** (⊠ 42 rue Dragon, 6ᵉ, ☎ 01–45–44–91–70,
métro St-Germain-des-Prés; ⊠ 25 rue Beaubourg 3ᵉ, ☎ 01–
42–74–72–40, métro Rambuteau) zeroes in on the season's hottest shoe styles and replicates them at prices 30%
cheaper than you'll find elsewhere in the city.

**Stéphane Kélian** (⊠ 23 bd. de la Madeleine, 1ᵉʳ, ☎ 01–42–96–01–84, métro Madeleine; ⊠ 6 Pl. des Victoires, 2ᵉ, ☎ 01–42–61–60–74, métro Bourse, Palais-Royal) creates chic, high-style shoes for men and women.

## Toys

**Au Nain Bleu** (⊠ 408 rue St-Honoré, 8ᵉ, ☎ 01–42–60–39–01, métro Concorde) is a high-priced wonderland of elaborate dollhouses, miniature sports cars, and enchanting hand-carved rocking horses.

# FRENCH VOCABULARY

One of the trickiest French sounds to pronounce is the nasal final *n* sound (whether or not the *n* is actually the last letter of the word). You should try to pronounce it as a sort of nasal grunt—as in "huh." The vowel that precedes the *n* will govern the vowel sound of the word, and in this list we precede the final *n* with an *h* to remind you to be nasal.

Another problem sound is the ubiquitous but untransliterable *eu*, as in *bleu* (blue) or *deux* (two), and the very similar sound in *je* (I), *ce* (this), and *de* (of). The closest equivalent might be the vowel sound in "put," but rounded.

## Words and Phrases

| English | French | Pronunciation |
|---|---|---|
| **Basics** | | |
| Yes/no | Oui/non | wee/nohn |
| Please | S'il vous plaît | seel voo play |
| Thank you | Merci | mair-see |
| You're welcome | De rien | deh ree-ehn |
| That's all right | Il n'y a pas de quoi | eel nee ah pah de kwah |
| Excuse me, sorry | Pardon | pahr-dohn |
| Sorry! | Désolé(e) | day-zoh-lay |
| Good morning/ afternoon | Bonjour | bohn-zhoor |
| Good evening | Bonsoir | bohn-swahr |
| Goodbye | Au revoir | o ruh-vwahr |
| Mr. (Sir) | Monsieur | muh-syuh |
| Mrs. (Ma'am) | Madame | ma-dam |
| Miss | Mademoiselle | mad-mwa-zel |
| Pleased to meet you | Enchanté(e) | ohn-shahn-tay |
| How are you? | Comment allez-vous? | kuh-mahn-tahl-ay voo |
| Very well, thanks | Très bien, merci | tray bee-ehn, mair-see |
| And you? | Et vous? | ay voo? |

## Numbers

| | | |
|---|---|---|
| one | un | uhn |
| two | deux | deuh |

| three | trois | twah |
| four | quatre | *kaht*-ruh |
| five | cinq | sank |
| six | six | seess |
| seven | sept | set |
| eight | huit | wheat |
| nine | neuf | nuf |
| ten | dix | deess |
| eleven | onze | ohnz |
| twelve | douze | dooz |
| thirteen | treize | trehz |
| fourteen | quatorze | kah-torz |
| fifteen | quinze | kanz |
| sixteen | seize | sez |
| seventeen | dix-sept | deez-*set* |
| eighteen | dix-huit | deez-*wheat* |
| nineteen | dix-neuf | deez-*nuf* |
| twenty | vingt | vehn |
| twenty-one | vingt-et-un | vehnt-ay-*uhn* |
| thirty | trente | trahnt |
| forty | quarante | ka-*rahnt* |
| fifty | cinquante | sang-*kahnt* |
| sixty | soixante | swa-*sahnt* |
| seventy | soixante-dix | swa-sahnt-*deess* |
| eighty | quatre-vingts | kaht-ruh-*vehn* |
| ninety | quatre-vingt-dix | kaht-ruh-vehn-*deess* |
| one hundred | cent | sahn |
| one thousand | mille | meel |

## Colors

| black | noir | nwahr |
| blue | bleu | bleuh |
| brown | brun/marron | bruhn/mar-*rohn* |
| green | vert | vair |
| orange | orange | o-*rahnj* |
| pink | rose | rose |
| red | rouge | rouge |
| violet | violette | vee-o-*let* |
| white | blanc | blahnk |
| yellow | jaune | zhone |

# Days of the Week

| | | |
|---|---|---|
| Sunday | dimanche | dee-*mahnsh* |
| Monday | lundi | luhn-*dee* |
| Tuesday | mardi | mahr-*dee* |
| Wednesday | mercredi | mair-kruh-*dee* |
| Thursday | jeudi | zhuh-*dee* |
| Friday | vendredi | vawn-druh-*dee* |
| Saturday | samedi | sahm-*dee* |

# Months

| | | |
|---|---|---|
| January | janvier | zhahn-vee-*ay* |
| February | février | feh-vree-*ay* |
| March | mars | marce |
| April | avril | a-*vreel* |
| May | mai | meh |
| June | juin | zhwehn |
| July | juillet | zhwee-*ay* |
| August | août | ah-*oo* |
| September | septembre | sep-*tahm*-bruh |
| October | octobre | awk-*to*-bruh |
| November | novembre | no-*vahm*-bruh |
| December | décembre | day-*sahm*-bruh |

# Useful Phrases

| | | |
|---|---|---|
| Do you speak English? | Parlez-vous anglais? | par-lay *voo* *ahn*-glay |
| I don't speak . . . French | Je ne parle pas . . . français | zhuh nuh parl pah frahn-*say* |
| I don't understand | Je ne comprends pas | zhuh nuh kohm-*prahn* pah |
| I understand | Je comprends | zhuh kohm-*prahn* |
| I don't know | Je ne sais pas | zhuh nuh say *pah* |
| I'm American/ British | Je suis américain/ anglais | zhuh sweez a-may-ree-*kehn*/ahn-glay |
| What's your name? | Comment vous ap-pelez-vous? | ko-mahn voo za-pell-ay-*voo* |
| My name is . . . | Je m'appelle . . . | zhuh ma-*pell* . . . |
| What time is it? | Quelle heure est-il? | kel air eh-*teel* |
| How? | Comment? | ko-*mahn* |
| When? | Quand? | kahn |
| Yesterday | Hier | yair |
| Today | Aujourd'hui | o-zhoor-*dwee* |

| | | |
|---|---|---|
| Tomorrow | Demain | duh-*mehn* |
| This morning/ afternoon | Ce matin/cet après-midi | suh ma-*tehn*/set ah-pray-mee-*dee* |
| Tonight | Ce soir | suh *swahr* |
| What? | Quoi? | kwah |
| What is it? | Qu'est-ce que c'est? | kess-kuh-*say* |
| Why? | Pourquoi? | *poor*-kwa |
| Who? | Qui? | kee |
| Where is . . . | Où est . . . | oo ay |
| the train station? | la gare? | la gar |
| the subway station? | la station de métro? | la sta-*syon* duh may-*tro* |
| the bus stop? | l'arrêt de bus? | la-*ray* duh *booss* |
| the terminal (airport)? | l'aérogare? | lay-ro-*gar* |
| the post office? | la poste? | la post |
| the bank? | la banque? | la bahnk |
| the . . . hotel? | l'hôtel . . .? | lo-*tel* |
| the store? | le magasin? | luh ma-ga-*zehn* |
| the cashier? | la caisse? | la *kess* |
| the . . . museum? | le musée . . .? | luh mew-*zay* |
| the hospital? | l'hôpital? | lo-pee-*tahl* |
| the elevator? | l'ascenseur? | la-sahn-*seuhr* |
| the telephone? | le téléphone? | luh tay-lay-*phone* |
| Where are the restrooms? | Où sont les toilettes? | oo sohn lay twah-*let* |
| Here/there | Ici/là | ee-*see*/la |
| Left/right | A gauche/à droite | a goash/a draht |
| Straight ahead | Tout droit | too drwah |
| Is it near/far? | C'est près/loin? | say pray/lwehn |
| I'd like . . . | Je voudrais . . . | zhuh voo-*dray* |
| a room | une chambre | ewn *shahm*-bruh |
| the key | la clé | la clay |
| a newspaper | un journal | uhn zhoor-*nahl* |
| a stamp | un timbre | uhn *tam*-bruh |
| I'd like to buy . . . | Je voudrais acheter . . . | zhuh voo-*dray* ahsh-tay |
| a cigar | un cigare | uhn see-*gar* |
| cigarettes | des cigarettes | day see-ga-*ret* |
| matches | des allumettes | days a-loo-*met* |
| dictionary | un dictionnaire | uhn deek-see-oh-*nare* |
| soap | du savon | dew sah-*vohn* |
| city map | un plan de ville | uhn plahn de *veel* |
| road map | une carte routière | ewn cart roo-tee-*air* |

| magazine | une revue | ewn reh-*vu* |
| envelopes | des enveloppes | dayz ahn-veh-*lope* |
| writing paper | du papier à lettres | dew pa-pee-*ay* a *let*-ruh |
| postcard | une carte postale | ewn cart pos-*tal* |
| How much is it? | C'est combien? | say comb-bee-*ehn* |
| It's expensive/ share | C'est cher/pas cher | say share/pa cheap |
| A little/a lot | Un peu/beaucoup | uhn peuh/bo-*koo* |
| More/less | Plus/moins | plu/mwehn |
| Enough/too (much) | Assez/trop | a-say/tro |
| I am ill/sick | Je suis malade | zhuh swee ma-*lahd* |
| Call a . . . | Appelez un . . . | a-play uhn |
| doctor | docteur | dohk-*tehr* |
| Help! | Au secours! | o suh-*koor* |
| Stop! | Arrêtez! | a-reh-*tay* |
| Fire! | Au feu! | o fuh |
| Caution!/Look out! | Attention! | a-tahn-see-*ohn* |

# Dining Out

| A bottle of . . . | une bouteille de . . . | ewn boo-*tay* duh |
| A cup of . . . | une tasse de . . . | ewn tass duh |
| A glass of . . . | un verre de . . . | uhn vair duh |
| Ashtray | un cendrier | uhn sahn-dree-*ay* |
| Bill/check | l'addition | la-dee-see-*ohn* |
| Bread | du pain | dew pan |
| Breakfast | le petit-déjeuner | luh puh-*tee* day-zhuh-*nay* |
| Butter | du beurre | dew burr |
| Cheers! | A votre santé! | ah vo-truh sahn-*tay* |
| Cocktail/aperitif | un apéritif | uhn ah-pay-ree-*teef* |
| Dinner | le dîner | luh dee-*nay* |
| Dish of the day | le plat du jour | luh plah dew *zhoor* |
| Enjoy! | Bon appétit! | bohn a-pay-*tee* |
| Fixed-price menu | le menu | luh may-*new* |
| Fork | une fourchette | ewn four-*shet* |
| I am diabetic | Je suis diabétique | zhuh swee dee-ah-bay-*teek* |
| I am on a diet | Je suis au régime | zhuh sweez oray-*jeem* |
| I am vegetarian | Je suis végé-tarien(ne) | zhuh swee vay-zhay-ta-ree-*en* |
| I cannot eat . . . | Je ne peux pas manger de . . . | zhuh nuh *puh* pah mahn-*jay* deh |
| I'd like to order | Je voudrais commander | zhuh voo-*dray* ko-mahn-*day* |

| I'm hungry/thirsty | J'ai faim/soif | zhay fahm/swahf |
|---|---|---|
| Is service/the tip included? | Est-ce que le service est compris? | ess kuh luh sair-*veess* ay comb-*pree* |
| It's good/bad | C'est bon/mauvais | say bohn/mo-*vay* |
| It's hot/cold | C'est chaud/froid | say sho/frwah |
| Knife | un couteau | uhn koo-*toe* |
| Lunch | le déjeuner | luh day-zhuh-*nay* |
| Menu | la carte | la cart |
| Napkin | une serviette | ewn sair-vee-*et* |
| Pepper | du poivre | dew *pwah*-vruh |
| Plate | une assiette | ewn a-see-*et* |
| Please give me . . . | Donnez-moi . . . | doe-nay-*mwah* |
| Salt | du sel | dew sell |
| Spoon | une cuillère | ewn kwee-*air* |
| Sugar | du sucre | dew *sook*-ruh |
| Waiter!/Waitress! | Monsieur!/ Mademoiselle! | muh-*syuh*/ mad-mwa-*zel* |
| Wine list | la carte des vins | la cart day an |

# INDEX

## A

L'Absinthe (store), *111*
À la Mère de Famille (food store), *112*
Accessories, shopping for, *109*
Accommodations, *76–89*
in 1st Arrondissement, *78–79*
in 2nd Arrondissement, *79, 82*
in 3rd Arrondissement, *82*
in 4th Arrondissement, *82–83*
in 5th Arrondissement, *83–84*
in 6th Arrondissement, *84–85*
in 7th Arrondissement, *85–86*
in 8th Arrondissement, *86–87*
in 9th Arrondissement, *87*
in 12th Arrondissement, *87–88*
in 14th Arrondissement, *88*
in 16th Arrondissement, *88–89*
in 17th Arrondissement, *89*
Addresses, *xii*
Air travel, *xii–xiv*
Airport transfers, *xii–xiv*
Alain Ducasse ✕, *72*
Alcazar ✕, *66*
L'Ambroisie ✕, *64*
Amphithéâtre, *51*
Anacréon ✕, *70–71*
Androuët ✕, *68*
Angélina ✕, *21*
Antiques, shopping for, *110*
Arc de Triomphe, *11*
Archives Nationales, *30–31*
Arènes de Lutèce, *38*
L'Artisan Parfumeur (store), *109*
Arts, *91–93*. ☞ Museums and galleries
Astier ✕, *70*
L'Astor 🏨, *86*
Atelier Brancusi, *31*
Atelier Delacroix, *45*
Atelier Montparnasse 🏨, *85*
ATMs, *xx*
Au Bascou ✕, *61*
Au Bon Accueil ✕, *67*
Au Bon Marché (store), *104*
Au Camelot ✕, *70*

Au Nain Bleu (store), *113*
Au Père Tranquille ✕, *75*
Au Printemps (store), *104–105*
Au Trou Gascon ✕, *70*
Aux Bons Crus (wine bar), *75*
Aux Crus de Bourgogne ✕, *60*
Avenue Montaigne, *101*

## B

Les Bains (nightclub), *94*
Baracane ✕, *64–65*
Le Baron Rouge (wine bar), *75*
Bars and clubs, *94–95*
La Bastide Odéon ✕, *66*
Bastille, *30–37*
Le Bataclan (nightclub), *96*
Bateau-Lavoir, *53*
Bateaux Mouches, *17*
Bazar de l'Hôtel de Ville (store), *105*
Beaubourg (Centre Pompidou), *31*
Berluti (store), *110*
Berthillon ✕, *40*
Bibliothèque François Mitterrand, *38*
Bicycling, *98*
Bistrot d'Hubert, *71–72*
Bofinger ✕, *64*
Bois de Boulogne, *11, 14*
Bookstores, *110*
Bouffes du Nord (theater), *93*
Bourse, *25*
Bourse du Commerce, *20*
Brasserie Flo ✕, *69*
Brentano's (bookstore), *110*
Bretonnerie 🏨, *82*
Bristol (hotel bar), *95*
Britain. ☞ United Kingdom
Britannique 🏨, *79*
British travelers
customs and duties for, *xvii*
passports for, *xxii*
Budget shopping, *108*
Bus travel, *xiv*
Business hours, *xiv–xv*
La Butte Chaillot ✕, *73*
By Terry (store), *109*

**C**

Le Cabaret (nightclub), 94
Cabarets, 95
Café Beaubourg ✕, 75
Café Charbon ✕, 94
Café de la Paix ✕, 28
Café Marly ✕, 75
Cafés, 6, 75
Caisse Nationale des Monuments
   Historiques, 31
Campagne et Provence ✕, 65
Canadian Embassy, xviii
Canadian travelers
customs and duties for, xvi–xvii
passports for, xxii
Canal St-Martin, 25
Car rental, xv
Car travel, xv–xvi
Caron de Beaumarchais 🏨, 82
Cash machines, xx–xxi
Castex 🏨, 83
Catacombs, 50
Le Cave Augé (store), 112
Cemeteries
Montparnasse, 50
Père Lachaise, 27
Center for Contemporary Jewish
   Documentation, 34
Centre Pompidou (Beaubourg), 31
Chacok (store), 111
Champ de Mars, 17
Champs-Élysées, 14, 101–102
Chanel (store), 111
Channel Tunnel, xxv
Chapelle Expiatoire, 27
Chardenoux ✕, 69
Chartier ✕, 68–69
Charvet (store), 110
Les Chauffeurs ✕, 73
Chez Georges ✕, 61
Chez Jenny ✕, 61
Chez Maître Paul ✕, 66
Chez Michel ✕, 69
Chez Omar ✕, 61, 64
Chez René ✕, 65
Children, activities for
Arènes de Lutèce, 38
Bateaux Mouches, 17
Bois de Boulogne, 11, 14
Champ de Mars, 17
Grande Galerie de l'Évolution, 40

Jardin des Plantes, 40–41
Jardin des Tuileries, 15
Jardin du Luxembourg, 47
Musée Bricard, 35
Parc de la Villette, 29
Parc Monceau, 29
Tour Eiffel, 19
Christian Dior (store), 111
Christian Liaigre (store), 112
Christian Louboutin (store), 109
Churches, 6
classical concerts, 92
Cimetière du Montparnasse, 50
Cimetière Père Lachaise, 27
Cinémathèque Française (movie
   theater), 92–93
Cité de la Musique, 29, 91
Cité des Sciences et de l'Industrie,
   29
Classical music, 91–92
Climate, xxvi
Closerie des Lilas ✕, 50
Clothing, shopping for, 110–112
Colette (store), 111
Colonne de Juillet, 36
Comédie Française, 20, 93
Compagnie Française de l'Orient et
   de la Chine (store), 112
Le Comptoir (wine bar), 94
Conciergerie (prison), 38, 40
Conservatoire National des
   Techniques, 27
Contre-Allée ✕, 71
Cosmetics, shopping for, 109
Costes 🏨, 78
La Coupole ✕, 71
Crazy Horse (cabaret), 95
Credit cards, xxi
La Crémaillère ✕, 75
Currency, xxi
Currency exchange, xxi–xxii
Customs and duties, xvi–xviii

**D**

Dalí, Salvador, 53
Dance, 92
Dary's (store), 109
La Défense, 14
Department stores, 104–105, 108
Le Dépôt (nightclub), 94–95
Deux-Iles 🏨, 82–83

Dining. ☞ Restaurants
Dipaki (store), 110
Diptyque (store), 112
Discount passes, xviii
Du Pareil Au Même (store), 110

## E

École Nationale des Beaux-Arts, 45
Église de la Madeleine, 20–21
Église du Dôme, 46
Église St-Louis de Invalides, 46
Eiffel, Gustave, 19
Eiffel Tower, 19
18th Arrondissement
restaurants in, 74
8th Arrondissement
accommodations in, 86–87
restaurants in, 67–68
Electricity, xviii
11th Arrondissement
restaurants in, 69–70
L'Élysée Montmartre (nightclub), 94, 96
Les Élysées ✕, 67
Embassies, xviii
Emergencies, xv, xviii–xix
English-language booksellers, 110
L'Epicerie (store), 111
Espace Dali, 53
L'Espadon Bleu ✕, 66
Étoile-Péreire ▦, 89
Et Vous (store), 111

## F

Façonnable (store), 110
Familia ▦, 83
Faubourg St-Honoré, 102
La Fermette Marbeuf ✕, 68
Festival d'Art Sacré, 92
15th Arrondissement
restaurants in, 71–72
5th Arrondissement
accommodations in, 83–84
restaurants in, 65
Film, 92–93
1st Arrondissement
accommodations in, 78–79
restaurants in, 60, 75
Flea markets, 108
Fondation Cartier, 50
Food and wine, shopping for, 112
Forum des Halles, 21

14th Arrondissement
accommodations in, 88
restaurants in, 71
4th Arrondissement
accommodations in, 82–83
restaurants in, 64–65, 75
Le Fumoir (bar), 94

## G

Galerie Vivienne (shopping arcade), 109
Galeries Lafayette (store), 27, 105
Gardens. ☞ Parks and gardens
Gay and lesbian bars and clubs, 94–95
Géode (movie theater), 29
Gifts, shopping for, 112
Grand Hôtel de Bescançon , 79
Grand Hôtel Inter-Continental, 87
Grand Palais, 14–15
Le Grand Véfour ✕, 60
Grande Arche de La Défense, 14
Grande Galerie de l'Évolution, 40
Grande Halle, 29
Grandes Écoles ▦, 84
Great Britain. ☞ British travelers; United Kingdom
Le Grizzli ✕, 64
Guy Savoy ✕, 74

## H

Les Halles, 102
Health clubs, 98
Historic sites
Arc de Triomphe, 11
Arènes de Lutèce, 38
Bastille, 30–37
Chapelle Expiatoire, 27
Conciergerie (prison), 38, 40
Église de la Madeleine, 20–21
Église du Dôme, 46
Eiffel Tower, 19
Hôtel de Ville (city hall), 31, 34
Hôtel des Monnaies (mint), 46
Ile St-Louis, 40
Louvre, 15–16
Musée National du Moyen-Age, 41
Notre-Dame Cathedral, 41–42
Opéra Garnier, 27, 92
Palais Bourbon, 48
Place de la Concorde, 16–17
Place du 18-Juin-1940, 51–52

*Place Vendôme,* 24
*Sacré-Coeur,* 56
*St-Germain l'Auxerrois,* church of, 24
*St-Germain-des-Prés,* church of, 48
*St-Gervais-St-Protais,* church of, 36–37
*St-Séverin,* church of, 43–44
*Ste-Chapelle* (Holy Chapel), 43, 92
*Sorbonne,* 44
**Holidays,** *xix*
**Hospitals,** *xviii–xix*
**Hotel bars,** 95
**Hôtel Crillon** ⊞, 86
**Hôtel d'Aubusson** ⊞, 85
**Hôtel de L'Abbaye** ⊞, 84–85
**Hôtel de Noailles** ⊞, 79, 82
**Hôtel de Sully,** 31
**Hôtel de Ville** (city hall), 31, 34
**Hôtel des Invalides,** 45–46
**Hôtel des Monnaies** (mint), 46
**Hôtel Drouot,** 28
**Hôtel du 7e Art** ⊞, 83
**Hotels.** ☞ Accommodations
**Housewares, shopping for,** 112
**Hugo, Victor,** 36
**Hyatt Regency Paris-Madeleine** ⊞, 86–87

### I

**Il Vicolo** ✕, 65
**Ile St-Louis,** 40
**Institut de France,** 46–47
**Institut du Monde Arabe,** 40

### J

**Jacques Mélac** (wine bar), 75
**Jamin** ✕, 72
**Jardin Atlantique,** 51
**Jardin des Plantes,** 40–41
**Jardin des Tuileries,** 15
**Jardin du Luxembourg,** 47
**Jardin du Luxembourg** ⊞, 83
**Jazz clubs,** 95–96
**Jean-Paul Gaultier** (store), 111
**Jogging,** 98–99

### K

**Kiosque Théâtre,** 91

### L

**Lac Inférieur,** 14
**Lac Supérieur,** 14

**Lancaster** ⊞, 87
**Lapin Agile** (cabaret), 53
**Latour Maubourg** ⊞, 86
**Left Bank,** 102
**Lesbian and gay bars and clubs,** 94–95
**Libraries,** 38
**Lido** (cabaret), 95
**Lionel Hampton Jazz Club,** 96
**Lodging.** ☞ Accommodations
**Longchamp** (racetrack), 14
**Louvre,** 15–16, 102–103
**Louvre Forum** ⊞, 79
**Lutétia** (hotel bar), 95

### M

**Ma Bourgogne** ✕, 75
**Maison de Victor Hugo,** 36
**La Maison du Chocolat** (store), 112
**Man Ray** (nightclub), 94
**Marais,** 30–37, 103
**Marais Plus** ✕, 35
**Le Marché aux Puces St-Ouen** (market), 108
**Mariage Frères** ✕, 75
**Maria Luisa** (store), 111
**Markets,** 108–109
**Marks & Spencer** (store), 105
**Max Linder Panorama** (movie theater), 93
**Memorials.** ☞ Monuments and memorials
**Le Mère Catherine,** 56
**Métro,** *xix–xx*
**Meurice** ⊞, 78
**Michel Perry** (store), 109
**Money,** *xx–xxi*
**Monoprix** (store), 108
**Montalembert** ⊞, 85
**Montmarte,** 52–53
**Montparnasse,** 49–52
**Montparnasse cemetery,** 50
**Monuments and memorials**
*Mémorial de la Déportation,* 41
*Mémorial du Martyr Inconnu,* 34
**Mosquée,** 41
**Le Moulin à Vins** ✕, 74
**Moulin de la Galette,** 53, 55
**Moulin Rouge** (cabaret), 55, 95
**Movies,** 92–93
**Museums and galleries,** 6–7
*Archives Nationales,* 30–31

Atelier Brancusi, 31
Atelier Delacroix, 45
Beaubourg (Centre Pompidou), 31
Cité des Sciences et de l'Industrie, 29
Espace Dali, 53
Fondation Cartier, 50
Grande Galerie de l'Evolution, 40
Institut du Monde Arabe, 40
in Jardin des Plantes, 40
Louvre, 15–16
Maison Européenne de la
    Photographie, 34
Musée Bricard, 35
Musée Carnavalet, 35
Musée Cernuschi, 28
Musée Cognacq-Jay, 35
Musée d'Art et d'histoire du Judaïsme,
    34
Musée d'Art Moderne de la Ville de
    Paris, 17, 19
Musée de la Chasse et de la Nature, 35
Musée de la Marine, 19
Musée de la Mode, 21
Musée de la Monnaie, 46
Musée de la Musique, 29
Musé de la Opéra, 28
Musée de l'Armée, 45
Musée de l'Erotisme, 55
Musée de l'Homme, 19
Musée de l'Orangerie, 16
Musée de Montmarte, 55
Musée des Monuments Français, 19
Musée des Plans-Reliefs, 45–46
Musée d'Orsay, 47–48
Musée du Jeu de Paume, 16
Musée Entomologique, 40
Musée Guimet, 19
Musée Maillol, 47
Musée Minéralogique, 40–41
Musée National d'Art Moderne, 31
Musée National du Moyen-Age, 41
Musée Nissim de Camondo, 28
Musée Paléontologique, 40
Musée Picasso, 35–36
Musée Rodin, 48
Petit Palais, 14–15
**Musée d'Orsay Café** ✕, 48
**Music**
bars, 94–95
cabarets, 95
classical, 91–92

jazz clubs, 95–96
opera, 93
rock, pop, and world music venues, 96

# N

**Napoléon Bonaparte**, 15
**New Morning** (jazz club), 96
**Nightlife**, 94–96
**19th Arrondissement**
restaurants in, 74
**9th Arrondissement**
accommodations in, 87
restaurants in, 68–69
**Notre-Dame Cathedral**, 41–42,
    97
**Notre-Dame de Bonne-Nouvelle**,
    28
**Notre-Dame du Travail**, 51

# O

**Office de Tourisme de la Ville de
    Paris**, 16
**L'Olympia** (nightclub), 96
**L'Open Café** (nightclub), 95
**Opera**, 93
**Opéra Comique**, 93
**Opéra de la Bastille**, 36, 93
**Opéra Garnier**, 28, 92
**Outdoor activities and sports.** ☞
    Sports

# P

**Palais Bourbon**, 48
**Palais de Chaillot**, 19
**Palais de Justice**, 42
**Palais de l'Élysée**, 21
**Palais du Luxembourg**, 47
**Palais-Royal**, 21, 24, 102–103
**La Palette** ✕, 45
**Panoplie** (store), 110
**Panthéon**, 42
**Paradis Latin** (cabaret), 95
**Parc de la Villette**, 29
**Parc Monceau**, 29
**Parc Montsouris** 🖳, 88
**Paris-Vision** (ticket source), 91
**Parks and gardens**
Jardin Atlantique, 51
Jardin des Plantes, 40–41
Jardin des Tuileries, 15
Jardin du Luxembourg, 47

Passage des Panoramas (shopping arcade), *109*
Passage des Pavillons (shopping arcade), *109*
Passage Jouffroy (shopping arcade), *109*
Passports and visas, *xxii*
Passy-Victor Hugo, *103*
Patachou ✕, *56*
Paul Minchelli ✕, *67*
Le Pavillon Bastille ⌶, *87–88*
Pavillon de la Reine ⌶, *82*
Perfume, shopping for, *109*
Le Petit Journal (jazz club), *96*
Le Petit Opportun (jazz club), *96*
Petit Palais, *14–15*
Le Petit Rétro ✕, *73–74*
Philippe Detourbe ✕, *72*
Picasso, Pablo, *35–36*
Pierre Gagnaire ✕, *67*
Place Blanche, *55*
Place de Catalogne, *51*
Place de la Bastille, *36*
Place de la Concorde, *16–17*
Place de la République, *29*
Place des Abbesses, *55*
Place des Victoires, *24, 104*
Place des Vosges, *36*
Place du 18-Juin-1940, *51–52*
Place du Tertre, *56*
Place Georges-Pompidou, *31*
Place Jean-Baptiste Clément, *56*
Place Vendôme, *24, 103*
Pompidou Center, *31*
Pont de l'Archevêché, *42*
Pont Neuf (New Bridge), *43*
Port de Montreuil (market), *108*
Porte de Vanves (market), *108*
Prisunic (store), *108*
Prunier ✕, *73*
Le Pulp! (nightclub), *95*

**Q**

Queen (nightclub), *95*
Queen's Hôtel, *88–89*

**R**

Raspail-Montparnasse ⌶, *88*
Réciprogue (store), *111*
Relais Christine ⌶, *84*
Le Relais du Parc ✕, *73*

Relais St-Germain ⌶, *84*
Le Reminet ✕, *65*
Le Repaire de Cartouche ✕, *69*
Le Restaurant d'Eric Frechon ✕, *74*
Restaurant du Palais-Royal ✕, *60*
Restaurants, *6, 59–75*
cafés, *6, 75*
in 1st Arrondissement, *60*
in 2nd Arrondissement, *61*
in 3rd Arrondissement, *61, 64*
in 4th Arrondissement, *64–65*
in 5th Arrondissement, *65*
in 6th Arrondissement, *66*
in 7th Arrondissement, *66–67*
in 8th Arrondissement, *67–68*
in 9th Arrondissement, *68–69*
in 10th Arrondissement, *69*
in 11th Arrondissement, *69–70*
in 12th Arrondissement, *70*
in 13th Arrondissement, *70–71*
in 14th Arrondissement, *71*
in 15th Arrondissement, *71–72*
in 16th Arrondissement, *72–74*
in 17th Arrondissement, *74*
in 18th Arrondissement, *74*
in 19th Arrondissement, *74*
wine bars, *75*
Ritz ⌶, *78*
Ritz Hemingway Bar, *95*
Rock clubs, *96*
Rodin, Auguste, *48*
Roland Garros Stadium, *14*
Rollerblading, *99*
Rue de la Paix, *103*
Rue Etienne Marcel, *104*
Rue St-Honoré, *104*

**S**

Sabbia Rosa (store), *109*
Sacré-Coeur, *56*
St-Augustin, church of, *29*
St-Étienne-du-Mont, *43*
St-Eustache, church of, *24, 92*
St-Germain-des-Prés, church of, *48, 92*
St-Germain l'Auxerrois, church of, *24*
St-Gervais-St-Protais, church of, *36–37*
Saint James Paris ⌶, *88*
St-Julien-le-Pauvre, *43, 92*

St-Louis-en-l'Ile, *43, 92*
St-Nicolas des Champs, *30*
St-Paul-St-Louis, church of, *37*
St-Roch, church of, *24, 92*
St-Séverin, church of, *43–44*
St-Sulpice, church of, *48–49*
Ste-Chapelle (Holy Chapel), *43, 92*
Ste-Élisabeth, *30*
Salle Pleyel, *91*
Salon de Thé du Palais Royal, *75*
Salons de thé. ☞ Cafés
La Samaritaine (store), *105*
Sébillon ✕, *68*
**2nd Arrondissement**
*accommodations in, 79, 82*
*restaurants in, 61*
Sentou Galerie, *112*
**17th Arrondissement**
*accommodations in, 89*
*restaurants in, 74*
**7th Arrondissement**
*accommodations in, 85–86*
*restaurants in, 66–67, 75*
Shakespeare & Company
  (bookstore), *110*
Shoe Bizz (store), *112*
Shoes, shopping for, *112–113*
Shopping, *7, 100–113*
**16th Arrondissement**
*accommodations in, 88–89*
*restaurants in, 72–74*
**6th Arrondissement**
*accommodations in, 84–85*
*restaurants in, 66*
Sorbonne, *44*
Specialty stores, *109–112*
Sports, *98–99*
Square Igor-Stravinsky, *37*
Le Square Trousseau ✕, *70*
Stéphane Kélian (store), *113*
Studio 28 (movie theater), *56–57*
Swimming pools, *98*

**T**

Taillevent ✕, *68*
Tara Jarmon (store), *111*
Taxes, *xxii–xxiii*
Taxis, *xxiii*
Telephones, *xxiii–xxiv*
**10th Arrondissement**
*restaurants in, 69*
Le Terroir ✕, *71*

Theater, *93*
*discount tickets, 91*
Théâtre de la Bastille, *92*
Théâtre de la Huchette, *93*
Théâtre de la Ville, *92*
Théâtre de l'Odéon, *49, 93*
Théâtre des Champs-Élysées, *91*
Théâtre Libre, *57*
Théâtre Musical de Paris, *93*
**3rd Arrondissement**
*accommodations in, 82*
*restaurants in, 61, 64*
**13th Arrondissement**
*restaurants in, 70–71*
Le Timgad ✕, *74*
Timing the trip, *xxvi*
Tipping, *xxiv*
Tour Montparnasse, *52*
Le Tourville ☉, *85–86*
Toys, shopping for, *113*
Trains, *xxiv–xxv*
*Métro, xix–xx*
Transportation
*from airports, xii–xiii*
*by bus, xiv*
*car rental, xv*
*by Métro, xix–xx*
*by taxi, xxiii*
*train travel, xxiv–xxv*
**12th Arrondissement**
*accommodations in, 87–88*
*restaurants in, 70*

**U**

United Kingdom. ☞ British travelers
*air travel from, xii*
*embassy of, xviii*
*train travel from, xxv*
United States Embassy, *xviii*

**V**

Val de Grâce church, *52*
Le Vaudeville ✕, *61*
Vendôme ☉, *79*
Victoire (store), *111–112*
Le Vieux Bistro ✕, *64*
Le Vieux Colombier ✕, *75*
Village Voice (bookstore), *110*
Le Violon d'Ingres ✕, *66–67*
Virgin Megastore, *91*
Visas, *xxii*
Visitor information, *xxv–xxvi*

# W

Weather, *xxvi*
Le What's Up Bar, *94*
Wine bars, *75*

# Z

Zara (store), *112*
Zenith (nightclub), *96*

# NOTES

# NOTES

# NOTES

# NOTES

# NOTES

# NOTES

# Fodor's

## Looking for a different kind of vacation?

**Fodor's** makes it easy with a full line of specialty guidebooks to suit a variety of interests—from adventure to romance to language help.

**Fodor's.** For the world of ways you travel.